A Pocket Guide to Writing in History

A Pocket Guide to Writing in History

THIRD EDITION

Mary Lynn Rampolla

Trinity College

Bedford/St. Martin's   Boston ◆ New York

For Bedford/St. Martin's
History Editor: Katherine E. Kurzman
Developmental Editor: Laura Arcari
Production Editor: Coleen A. O'Hanley
Production Supervisor: Dennis J. Conroy
Director of Marketing: Karen Melton
Copyeditor: Rosemary Winfield
Text Design: Claire Seng-Niemoeller
Cover Design: Hannus Design Associates
Composition: Karla Goethe
Printing and Binding: Malloy Lithographing, Inc.

President: Charles H. Christensen
Editorial Director: Joan E. Feinberg
Director of Editing, Design, and Production: Marcia Cohen
Managing Editor: Elizabeth M. Schaaf

Library of Congress Control Number: 00-106488

Manufactured in the United States of America.

5   4   3   2   1
f   e   d   c   b

For information, write: Bedford/St. Martin's, 75 Arlington
Street, Boston, MA 02116 (617-399-4000)

ISBN: 0–312–24766–4

Acknowledgments

Excerpts from *France and the Dreyfus Affair: A Documentary History*
edited with an introduction by Michael Burns. Copyright © 1999
by Bedford/St. Martin's.

Metacrawler search results: Reprinted with the express consent of
Go2Net, Inc. All rights reserved.

Netscape screen: Netscape Communications Corporation has not
authorized, sponsored, endorsed, or approved this publication and
is not responsible for its content. Netscape and the Netscape
Communications Corporate Logos, are trademarks and trade names
of Netscape Communications Corporation. All other product names
and/or logos are trademarks of their respective owners.

Network Solutions banner advertisement: Copyright © Network
Solutions, Inc. All rights reserved.

Excerpt from *The Labyrinth of Exile: A Life of Theodor Herzl* by Ernst
Pawel. Copyright © 1989 by Ernst Pawel. Reprinted by permission
of Farrar, Straus & Giroux, LLC.

Photograph of Dreyfus's military degradation: Michael Burns
Private Collection.

Preface

For many students, the paper assigned in their first-year history survey is also their introduction to writing a college-level essay, a situation that they — and their instructors — may find less than satisfactory. Though many students understand that college papers must do more than restate information gleaned from lectures and books, they may have only a vague idea of how to go about researching, writing, and documenting a history paper. Instructors must convey a great deal of information about history and historical methodology in a limited amount of time, often in large lecture classes; thus, they can devote only very limited time specifically to writing instruction. *A Pocket Guide to Writing in History* is designed with just such situations in mind.

This book has undergone significant modifications since 1995. This new edition has been completely redesigned to make the book even easier to use, while maintaining the most valuable features of the first two editions. Like the earlier versions, *A Pocket Guide to Writing in History* is brief and accessible, and can be tucked into a pocket or a bookbag. It introduces students to the conventions of writing in history, provides an overview of typical assignments, and offers advice on research and using sources. It also includes abundant documentation models based on *The Chicago Manual of Style*. In this edition, however, our coverage of the computer as a tool for research and writing has been greatly expanded and enhanced. New features include advice on conducting an Internet search and evaluating Internet sources, tips on using spelling and grammar checkers, and an enlarged and updated list of Internet Resources in History. This new edition also incorporates revisions suggested by our users: The discussion of primary and secondary sources has been significantly expanded, including a new case study on working with primary and secondary sources; specific guidelines for evaluating primary, secondary, and Internet sources have been added; and a new section offers help for incorporating and citing nonwritten sources in history papers. This edition also includes an excerpt from a sample student paper, providing a model for a title page, introductory paragraph, endnotes, and bibliography.

v

While preparing this manuscript, I benefitted especially from the advice and encouragement of my colleagues and the suggestions of my students at Trinity College in Washington, D.C. I am especially indebted to the following historians for their thoughtful reviews of the second edition: Edward E. Baptist, University of Miami; Karl Barbir, Siena College; Mark Burkholder, University of Missouri; Stephen G. Fritz, East Tennessee State University; Reid A. Holland, Midlands Technical College; Katherine A. Hermes, Central Connecticut State University; Thomas Kay, Wheaton College; Gary J. Kornblith, Oberlin College; Bryan Lamkin, Azusa Pacific University; Dr. Diana J. Reynolds, Point Loma Nazarene Community College; Susan Schulten, University of Denver; Elizabeth Simmons-O'Neill, University of Washington.

At Bedford/St. Martin's, I would like to thank Chuck Christensen, president, and Joan Feinberg, editorial director, who conceived the idea for this book. I would also like to thank my editor, Laura Arcari; Elizabeth Schaaf, the managing editor; Katherine Kurzman, the sponsoring editor; Coleen O'Hanley, the production editor; Jamie Farrell for clearing the permissions; Amy McConathy for updating the documentation models; and Rosemary Winfield, the copyeditor.

Finally, I would like to thank Susan Craig, director of the Sr. Helen Sheehan Library at Trinity College, who compiled the detailed, up-to-date list of research sources that concludes this manual.

Mary Lynn Rampolla
Trinity College
Washington, D.C.

Contents

A Pocket Guide
to Writing
in History

1

Introduction:
Why Study History?

On the old television police series *Dragnet,* Sergeant Joe
Friday curbed the speculations of his witnesses with a stern
admonition: "Just the facts, Ma'am. Just the facts."
Students who take their first college history class with a
sense of foreboding often think that historians, like Joe
Friday, are interested only in compiling lists of names,
dates, places, and "important" events that happened
sometime in the past. But history is much more than this.
The historian's goal is to acquire insight into the ideas
and realities that shaped the lives of men and women
of earlier societies. Some of the beliefs and institutions of
the past may seem alien to us; others are all too familiar.
But in either case, when we study the people of the past,
what we are really learning about is the rich diversity
of human experience. The study of history is the study of
the beliefs and desires, practices and institutions, of human
beings.

Why should you bother studying the past in our
increasingly future-oriented society? First of all, a
thoughtful examination of the past can tell us a great deal
about how we came to be who we are. When we study
history, we are looking at the roots of modern institutions,
ideas, values, and problems. Second, the effort you put
into grappling with the assumptions and world views of
earlier societies teaches you to see the world through
different eyes. The ability to perceive and recognize the
meaning of events from a perspective other than your own
and to appreciate the diversity of human beliefs and
cultures is of inestimable value in our increasingly complex
and multicultural society. Moreover, an awareness of
various perspectives encourages students of history to
engage in a critical analysis of their own culture and society
and to recognize and critique their own assumptions.

History is a complex discipline, and historians are a diverse group. They take different approaches to their material; they interpret the events of the past in different ways; they even disagree on such basic issues as whether and to what extent historians can be objective. Regardless of their approaches, however, historians see writing as an important tool of inquiry and communication.

In addition to introducing you to some of the basic elements of what historians do, this manual provides guidelines for writing papers in the field of history. Of course, the vast majority of students enrolled in their first history course are not contemplating a career in history. Indeed, most history majors follow career paths that lead them away from the study of the past into fields like law, government, business, and international relations. Nevertheless, the techniques you will need to master to write an effective history paper — how to read critically, think analytically, argue persuasively, and write clearly — are skills that will be useful to you wherever your academic interests take you and that you will value in whatever career path you choose to follow.

1a. Historical questions

Historians come to their work with a deep curiosity about the past; to satisfy that curiosity, they ask questions. It has been suggested that historians are like detectives; it is certainly true that they ask some of the same questions: *Who? What? When? Where?* and *Why?* Some of these questions are designed to elicit "the facts" and are relatively easy to answer: *Who* was the emperor of Japan during World War II? *What* tools did eighteenth-century weavers use? *When* did the Vietnamese drive the Khmer Rouge out of Phnom Penh? *Where* did the first Continental Congress meet? Other questions, however, are less easy to answer: *Who* was Jack the Ripper? *What* were the religious beliefs of the peasants of twelfth-century Languedoc? *When* did President Nixon learn about the Watergate break-in? *Where* did the inhabitants of the original settlement at Roanoke go, and *why* did they disappear? More complex questions such as these have formed the basis of absorbing historical studies.

Historians also ask questions that help them analyze relationships between historical facts. Many of the questions historians ask, for example, reflect their interest in understanding the **context** in which the events of the past occurred. For example, a historian interested in the scientific revolution of the seventeenth century would not simply write about scientific "advances," such as Copernicus's theory that the sun, and not the earth, was the center of the solar system. Rather, the historian would also ask questions about historical context: What role did political issues play in the acceptance or rejection of Copernicus's theory? Why did some theologians find his ideas threatening to religion, while others did not? What impact did larger social, political, and intellectual movements, like Renaissance humanism or the Reformation, have on the study of astronomy in this period? In other words, historians do not examine events in isolation; rather, they try to understand the people and events of the past in terms of the unique historical context that helped to shape them.

As they explore the relationships between and among events in the past, historians also ask about the **causes** of events. The historical events that you will be studying and writing about can almost never be traced to a single cause, and historians are careful to avoid simplistic cause-and-effect relationships as explanations for events. For example, although the assassination of Archduke Franz Ferdinand was the event that precipitated World War I, no historian would argue that it *caused* the war. Rather, historians try to uncover the complex multiplicity of causes that grow out of the historical context in which events occurred.

Historians also ask questions about the relationship between **continuity** (events, conditions, ideas, and so on that remain the same over time) and **change.** Many of the questions historians ask reflect this interest. For example, a historian who asks "What impact did the Black Death have on the economic and legal status of the peasants?" is interested in examining the changes brought about by the bubonic plague against the backdrop of the ongoing institution of serfdom.

Finally, while the past doesn't change, historians' interests — and the questions they ask — do. Historians, like the people they study, are part of a larger context. They are guided in their choice of subject and in their questions by their own interests and by the interests and concerns of their societies. As they ask new questions, historians look at sources in new ways. They may even discover "new" sources — sources that had always existed but had been ignored or dismissed as irrelevant. History, therefore, is a vital and dynamic discipline. We will never know all there is to know about the past because we are constantly posing new questions, and our questions, in turn, help us to see the past in new ways.

The best way to enter the world of the historian is to ask as many questions as you can about the particular historical issues you are studying. As you seek the answers to your questions, be aware of the new and more complex questions that your answers raise, and let them guide your exploration further.

1b. Historical sources

To answer their questions, historians evaluate, organize, and interpret a wide variety of sources. These sources fall into two broad categories: *primary sources* and *secondary sources*. To study history and write history papers, you will need to know how to work with both kinds of sources.

1b-1. Primary sources

Primary sources are materials produced by people or groups directly involved in the event or topic under consideration, either as participants or as witnesses. Examples of primary sources include eyewitness accounts, decrees, letters and diaries, newspapers and magazines, speeches, auto-biographies, and treatises. Tax rolls, census data, and marriage, birth, and death registers are also primary sources. In addition, historians sometimes examine primary sources that are not written — like coins, works of art, films, recordings, or archaeological remains. For recent history, oral sources, such as interviews with World War II veterans or Holocaust survivors, can also be primary sources. By examining primary sources, historians gain insights into the thoughts, behaviors, and experiences of the people of the past.

When using a written primary source, it is important to *read the source itself*. Do not simply rely on another historian's analysis of the source. The purpose of writing history, after all, is to develop your *own* interpretation based on the evidence you have assembled. If possible, you should read the whole source rather than excerpts from a reader. When you are writing a history paper, you need to know the *significance* of the entire document and the context of any portions of the source that you wish to discuss or quote. Moreover, in the process of choosing excerpts, an editor is making a judgment about what aspects of the source are important. In effect, he or she is determining the significance of the source for you. However, sources can yield different kinds of information depending on the questions the historian asks; therefore, it is preferable to read primary sources in their entirety.

1b-2. Secondary sources

Historians also use *secondary sources:* books and articles in scholarly journals that comment on and interpret primary sources. Secondary sources are extremely useful. Reading secondary sources is often the simplest and quickest way to become informed about what is already known about the subject you are studying. In addition, reading scholarly books and articles will inform you about the ways in which other historians have understood and interpreted events. Finally, secondary sources can be an important research tool. Reading them carefully can help you find a subject for a research paper by pointing you toward topics that have not yet been explored fully or about which there is controversy. Moreover, the bibliographies of secondary sources can direct you to primary sources. As valuable as they are, however, you should never base a history paper entirely on secondary sources. Whenever possible, you should study the events of the past in the words of people who experienced, witnessed, or participated in them.

1b-3. Primary or secondary?

The status of a source as primary or secondary depends on the question you ask. If you are writing about the reign of Richard III (1483–85), your primary sources might include edicts, chronicles composed by contemporary witnesses to the events of his reign, and letters written by foreign ambassadors to the English court. Strictly speaking, Thomas More's *History of Richard III,* written in the early sixteenth century, would be a secondary source because More was not a witness to the events he describes, and he records only the evidence provided to him by others. If, however, you are writing about the depiction of Richard III in the early Tudor period, More would be a primary source.

1b-4. Analyzing and interpreting sources

If sources always told the truth, the historian's job would
be much easier — and also rather boring. But sources, like
witnesses in a murder case, often lie. Sometimes they lie
on purpose, telling untruths to further a specific
ideological, philosophical, or political agenda. Sometimes
they lie by omission, leaving out bits of information that
are crucial to interpreting an event. Sometimes sources
mislead unintentionally because the author was not aware
of all the facts, misinterpreted the facts, or was misin-
formed. Many are biased, either consciously or
unconsciously, and contain unstated assumptions; all
reflect the interests and concerns of their authors. In any
case, historians' sources often conflict; two different
sources may tell two very different stories. As a result, one
of the challenges you will face in writing a history paper
is evaluating the reliability and usefulness of your sources.

One way in which historians evaluate primary sources
is to compare them; a fact or description contained in
one source is more likely to be accepted as trustworthy if
other sources support or corroborate it. Another technique
historians use to evaluate the reliability of a source is to
identify the author's biases. We might be less inclined,
for example, to believe Polydore Vergil's assertion that
Richard III killed his nephews if we realize that he was the
official court historian for Henry VII, who killed Richard
in battle and seized the throne for himself. Historians also
read their sources carefully for evidence of internal
contradictions or logical inconsistencies, and they pay
attention to their sources' use of language, since the
adjectives and metaphors an author uses can point to
hidden biases and unspoken assumptions.

Secondary sources may also contradict each other.
Several historians can examine the same set of materials
and interpret them in very different ways. Similarly,
historians can try to answer the same questions by looking
at different kinds of evidence or by using different methods
to gather, evaluate, and interpret evidence. You can use
the same techniques to evaluate a secondary source as you
would use to evaluate a primary source. Compare your
source with other secondary sources, identify biases and
unconscious assumptions, and look for logical
inconsistencies. Most important, however, you should
return wherever possible to the primary sources and
consider whether the author uses and interprets the

sources appropriately. The study of the ways in which historians have interpreted the past is called *historiography,* and knowing how to read and evaluate the work of other historians is so important that some professors may ask you to write a historiographic essay (see pp. 27–28). In any case, to get the most out of your reading of secondary sources, you will need to study a variety of interpretations of historical events and issues and learn how to read carefully and critically. (For a fuller discussion on evaluating sources, see pp. 13–20, "Reading Critically.")

1b-5. Looking at historical sources: An example

Much of the excitement in studying history comes from working with a wide variety of source materials. The following three primary sources (two written texts and a photograph) and one secondary source all pertain to the Dreyfus affair, one of the most infamous episodes in nineteenth-century French history. Taken as a group, they illustrate some of the challenges — and pleasures — of working with historical sources.

Captain Alfred Dreyfus was a Jewish artillery officer in the French army. In 1894, he was accused of high treason, condemned by a court-martial, and sentenced to life at the Devil's Island penal colony off the coast of French Guiana. From the beginning, the evidence against Dreyfus was flimsy, and the proceedings were tainted by anti-Semitism. In 1898, a scathing indictment by Emile Zola, one of the most prominent French novelists of his time, forced the military to reopen the case. Dreyfus was officially pardoned and ultimately exonerated in the court of public opinion.

The Dreyfus affair raises historically significant questions about a wide variety of issues: the role of the military in late nineteenth-century French society; the character and importance of anti-Semitism in Europe; even the role of the media in forming and re-forming public opinion. Historians have therefore been drawn to the sources that can help them understand and interpret the Dreyfus affair.

The following documents, which can be found in Michael Burns's *France and the Dreyfus Affair: A Documentary History* (Bedford/St. Martin's, 1999), are all related to a single event in the history of the Dreyfus affair:

the degradation ceremony, in which Dreyfus was formally stripped of his military rank and insignia.

Document 1 is an account of the degradation by Leon Daudet, a French journalist writing for *Le Figaro* (Burns, 51–52):

> The fatal door opens on the hideous cortege: four artillerymen and, between them, the criminal; close by, the executioner, a sergeant major of the Republican Guard . . . . Quickly, the executioner, a sort of helmeted giant, approaches the condemned man, a rigid and dark silhouette on which all attention is focused. Without an instant of hesitation, the executioner goes for the military cap; he tears off the insignia, the fine gold braids, the ornaments of the jacket and sleeves. The dumb puppet prepares himself for the atrocious work; he even lifts his arms. He shouts a few words — "Innocent! . . . Innocent! . . . Long live France! . . ." — which hardly carry through the heavy, anguish-filled atmosphere . . . . I catch a glimpse of the condemned man's wan and weasel-like face, raised up in final defiance . . . . The giant takes the sword of the man who had been a captain and, with a final sharp, lightning blow, breaks it over his knee . . . . What more can one do with this little automaton, completely black and stripped of everything, with this hideous beast of treason who remains upright on his rigid limbs, survivor of his own catastrophe . . . ?

Document 2 is an account of the same event written by Theodor Herzl, a correspondent for Austria's *Neue Freie Presse* (Burns 54, 57):

> . . . Dreyfus was led out wearing the uniform of a captain. Four soldiers brought him before the general, who declared, "Alfred Dreyfus, you are unworthy to bear arms. I hereby degrade you in the name of the French people. Let the judgment be executed." Thereupon Dreyfus raised his right hand and shouted: "I swear and declare that you are degrading an innocent man. Vive la France." With that, the drums began to roll, and the military bailiff tore the already loosened buttons and straps from the uniform. Dreyfus maintained his proud bearing, and the procedure was completed within a few minutes . . . . Now began the ordeal of filing past the troops. Dreyfus marched like a man convinced of his innocence . . . . The strangely resolute attitude of the degraded captain made a deep impression on many eyewitnesses.

Document 3 is a photograph of the event. Dreyfus is standing erect before the blurred figure of the bailiff, who is in the act of breaking Dreyfus's sword over his knees (Burns, 55).

Figure 1.1   Photograph of Dreyfus's military degradation

An observant reader would notice immediately that, while the three primary sources purport to record the same event, they represent three distinctive views of that event. In working with these documents, then, the student would need to determine the biases and perspectives that each source represents. Who are the authors of the two articles? For whom were they writing? Does the French journalist present a different perspective than the Austrian, who, as a foreigner, would see the event as an "outsider"? Did either of them write other articles about Dreyfus or the French military, and if so, what views did these articles express? What do we know about the newspapers Daudet and Herzl represented? Were they liberal or conservative? Who comprised the general readership of these papers, and what political, social, or economic groups did they represent? What kinds of biases are revealed in the sources? What words do they use to describe Dreyfus, the crowd, and the ritual? How should your awareness of these biases affect the way you read the texts? Does the photograph support or contradict specific elements of the written accounts? Was the photograph published, and, if so, where? How does each source depict Dreyfus's appearance and behavior? Do the sources agree on any details that would enable us to determine "what happened"? Where do the sources disagree, and what is the significance of these contradictions? Finally, are there any additional related sources to which these should be compared?

Michael Burns, the author of the book in which these documents appear, addresses these and other issues of historical interpretation in his commentary, which constitutes a secondary source for these events (Burns, 51, 53, 57):

> Recounted in newspaper reports, diaries, memoirs, and illustrations, as well as in a handful of rare photographs, Dreyfus's public degradation, punctuated by shouts of "Death to the Jew!" became a touchstone of memory for many of those who witnessed or read about the ten-minute ritual of humiliation . . . . For journalist Leon Daudet, it marked an orgy of revenge against a "wretched" Jew. Laced with hatred and crafted with skill, Daudet's account . . . stands as one of the affair's most notorious monuments. . . . Another journalist reported on the degradation for the Austrian newspaper *Neue Freie Presse*. Only a few months later, Theodor Herzl, a Viennese Jew on assignment in Paris since 1891, would complete the first draft of *Der Judenstaat* (The Jewish State) and at decade's end would declare that "the Dreyfus case made me a Zionist." . . . But the "terrible and significant" lessons Herzl learned from the Dreyfus case seemed to have crystallized over the months following the degradation . . . . The visual images of the degradation — the quick sketches and elaborate lithographs aimed at a wide audience in Paris and provincial towns — often repeated the same inaccuracies found in newspaper reports and editorials . . . . *Le Quotidien illustre* carried a portrait of the "traitor" with head bowed and body stooped in defeat. Soon to become an icon of the affair, it depicted a moment that never happened. And a photograph, taken from a distant window of Ecole Militaire, proved the point. While "the executioner," a ghostlike blur, breaks Dreyfus's sword, the captain . . . stands straight, his head held high.

While primary documents are essential to the historian's work, this secondary source is extremely useful for the student in two ways. First of all, it illustrates some of the ways in which historians analyze source materials. For example, Burns places these three sources in their context, noting that they are part of a much larger group of texts and visual images, published and unpublished, that record the event under consideration. He provides information about the identity of the authors of the texts and analyzes the ways in which their biases and viewpoints affected their interpretation. In addition, he places the event itself in a broader historical context, noting the importance of Dreyfus's military degradation as a symbol or a "touchstone of memory." Finally, this text also models the ways in which one historical source (the photograph) can be used to judge the validity of other sources.

Second, Burns's analysis illustrates some of the ways in which secondary sources can be useful to students in their attempts to engage in historical study. Burns provides the reader with important information about the authors of the texts that is not immediately apparent from the texts themselves. For example, we learn that Herzl was a Jew and was profoundly affected by Dreyfus's degradation. Armed with this knowledge, the student could return to the primary sources with new questions: Did Herzl's religious affiliation affect his experience of Dreyfus's degradation? What connections did Herzl have with the Zionist movement prior to this event, and how did his views about Zionism change as a result of the trial?

Reading good secondary sources, then, is not just a way to gather information. Rather, secondary sources can provide you with models for conducting your own historical research and send you back to the primary sources with fresh perspectives and new questions of your own.

These primary and secondary documents illustrate some of the complexity — and excitement — of the historian's craft. As you read and analyze primary sources, critique the interpretations of secondary sources, and develop historical interpretations of your own, you will gain essential critical skills.

1c. How this manual can help you

When you do research and writing in a history course, you will become a participant in historical debate. As you devise questions about historical topics and seek answers in primary and secondary sources, you will begin to come to conclusions about those topics. In the papers you write for your history courses, you will construct arguments about those conclusions and offer support for them. This manual will help you understand the process from start to finish. After introducing typical assignments in history, the manual describes conventions of writing that are specific to the discipline. It then discusses how to use sources effectively. Finally, it explains how to give proper credit to those sources.

History, like the other arts and sciences, provides a window onto the ideas and beliefs, the actions and passions, of human beings. Reading and writing history entail above all an exploration of who and what we are. This manual is designed to aid you in such exploration and to help you discover the pleasures of studying history.

2
Approaching Typical Assignments in History

The reading and writing projects assigned to you in a history course will give you opportunities to learn more about historical issues, events, and people and also to act as a historian by contributing your own ideas to the field. This section begins with a discussion of critical reading. Reading is, after all, the assignment you will encounter most frequently in your history courses. This is followed by a review of the most common types of short writing assignments you might encounter — ranging from summaries, book reviews, and annotated bibliographies to short papers and historiographic essays — with suggestions for some general ways of approaching these assignments. The section ends with a discussion of essay exams.

NOTE: Many professors include detailed instructions with their writing assignments. You should always read these instructions carefully, follow them closely, and ask for further explanation if you do not fully understand them. The suggestions here are meant to complement your professor's guidelines, not in any way to replace them.

2a. Reading critically

History courses typically require a great deal of reading from a wide variety of sources. If your professor has assigned a textbook, you will probably be expected to read a chapter or two each week. You may also be asked to read a variety of secondary sources, including articles from scholarly journals or books about a particular aspect of your topic. Many professors also assign primary sources, documents ranging from medieval chronicles to legal documents to newspaper accounts. (For a fuller discussion of the types of documents historians use, see pp. 4–7). Furthermore, if you are writing a research paper, you will need to find, read, and analyze a variety of sources pertaining to your topic that are not part of the reading assigned to the whole class.

Since reading is such an important assignment, it is essential to give serious consideration to *how* you read. Reading for a history course is not like reading a novel; it is not enough to skim each page once and get the gist of the story. In fact, as you do your reading assignments, you must accomplish several tasks: You need not only to *understand* the content of what you are reading but also to *analyze* its significance, *evaluate* its usefulness, and *synthesize* all of your reading into one coherent picture of the topic you are studying. Careful and critical reading is crucial both for active and intelligent participation in class discussion and for writing effective papers. This is true, of course, whether you are reading printed or online texts.

The best way to become a careful and critical reader is to become an *active* reader, constantly asking questions of the texts you are reading.

2b. Evaluating sources

The questions that you pose of your sources depend in part on the nature of the sources you are working with.

Both primary and secondary sources can provide valuable information; however, they provide different kinds of information. If you are studying nineteenth-century communes, for example, primary sources such as the diaries or letters of commune members can provide firsthand information about the thoughts, feelings, and daily lives of the people who lived in them. Primary sources would be less useful, however, in helping you understand the larger, sociological effects of communal living. To get a better understanding of those effects, you might turn to secondary sources in which historians offer a broader perspective on communes, perhaps examining several such communities over time. (See pp. 4–7 for a fuller discussion of primary and secondary sources.)

2b-1. Evaluating primary sources

Primary sources form the basic material of the historian. Nevertheless, historians do not take the evidence provided by such sources simply at face value. Like good detectives, they evaluate the evidence, approaching their sources analytically and critically.

Since primary sources originate in the period you are studying, you might be inclined to trust what they say implicitly. After all, if the author is an eyewitness, why should you doubt his or her word? However, as any police investigator could tell you, eyewitnesses see different things and remember them in different ways. The previous section noted some issues that you should take into consideration in evaluating primary sources (see pp. 4–7). In general, when you deal with primary sources, you should always ask the following:

- Who is the author?
- Why did he or she write the source?
- Who was the intended audience?
- What unspoken assumptions does the text contain?
- Are there detectable biases in the source?
- When was the source composed?
- What is the historical context in which the source was written and read?
- Are there other contemporary sources to compare against this one?

EVALUATING PRIMARY SOURCES: AN EXAMPLE. In a letter written to Sheik El-Messiri in 1798, Napoleon expresses the hope that the sheik will soon establish a government in Egypt based on the principles of the Qu'ran, the sacred text of Islam. Those principles, according to Napoleon, "alone are true and capable of bringing happiness to men."[1] Should we assume, on the evidence of this letter, that Napoleon believed in the truth of Islam? A historian might ask, "Do we have any other evidence for Napoleon's attitude toward Islam?" "What do other primary sources tell us about Napoleon's attitude toward religions such as Catholicism, Protestantism, and Judaism?" "Do any other primary sources contradict the attitude toward Islam

1. Napoleon Bonaparte, "Letter to the Sheik El-Messiri," in *The Mind of Napoleon: A Selection from His Written and Spoken Words*, 4th ed., trans. and ed. J. Christopher Herold (New York: Columbia University Press, 1969), 104.

expressed in Napoleon's letter to the sheik?" In other words, "How accurately and to what extent can this source answer questions about Napoleon's religious beliefs?" In addition, historians try to understand or interpret their sources even if those sources do not offer the best or most accurate information on a certain topic. As it happens, Napoleon did not believe in Islam. This does not mean, however, that his letter to the sheik should be relegated to the dustbin. Instead, a good historian will ask, "Under what circumstances did Napoleon write this letter?" "Who was Sheik El-Messiri, and what was his relationship to Napoleon?" "What does this letter tell us about Napoleon's willingness to use religion to his political advantage?" Thus, to write about historical questions, you will need to know how to approach many different kinds of primary sources and ask appropriate questions of them.

THINKING ABOUT EDITIONS AND TRANSLATIONS. When professional historians work with primary sources, they travel to archives and libraries around the world to work directly with the original letters, manuscripts, photographs, and so on that make up their primary sources. When they turn to published editions of their sources, either in print or online, they work with these sources in their original languages. Undergraduates rarely have the time, the opportunity, or the linguistic skills to conduct this kind of research. Instead, students rely on published editions of primary sources in translation or, increasingly, on documents posted on the Internet, which is an excellent source for a wide variety of documents, photographs, and other primary materials.

Using modern editions of sources in translation is an excellent way to enter into the world view of the people you are studying. Nevertheless, you should be aware that any edited text reflects, to some extent, the interests and experiences of the editor or translator. For example, in the "Autobiographical Postscript" to his edition of *Gilgamesh,* Herbert Mason reveals that he was profoundly affected by the death of his father, an event that influenced his interpretation of the epic poem. Similarly, as noted earlier (p. 5), the process by which the editor of a document collection selects which documents to include and which to leave out also involves *interpretation*. The collection, as it appears in print, reflects how the editor interprets and organizes the material and what he or she sees as significant. The following suggestions will help you use both print and online sources most effectively:

- Always read the preface and introduction carefully to determine the principles underlying the editor's process of selection.
- Pay careful attention to the footnotes or endnotes, which will alert you to alternate readings or translations of the material in the text.
- When using an online source, follow the links that lead you to further sources or information.
- As a rule, use the most recent edition, which reflects the current state of scholarship.

NOTE FOR INTERNET USERS. The Internet is an excellent source for many primary materials. Nevertheless, it is important to remember that to abide by copyright laws, some Web sites, particularly those dealing with older materials, may post translations of sources that are in the "public domain." (A reputable Web site will inform you if this is the case.) Translations that are in the public domain were made so long ago that they are no longer covered by copyright restrictions. In such a case, the Internet is still an extremely useful tool for making you aware of the wide variety of sources that are available, but once you find a source you intend to use, you will probably want to look for the most recent printed edition or translation.

2b-2. Evaluating secondary sources

Reading secondary sources helps you understand how other historians have interpreted the primary sources for the period you are studying. Students sometimes hesitate to question the conclusions of established scholars; nevertheless, as with primary sources, it is important to read secondary sources critically and analytically.

You should ask of secondary sources the same questions you ask of primary sources:

- Who is the author?
- Why did he or she write this text?
- Who is the intended audience?
- Does the text contain any unspoken assumptions or detectable biases?

In addition, the following questions are especially important to think about when you use a secondary source.

WHEN WAS THE SOURCE PUBLISHED? If it is important that you know the most recent theories about a historical subject, you should pay special attention to the publication dates of the sources you are considering. A 1999 article reviewing theories about construction of Native American burial mounds may contain more recent ideas than a 1964 review. You should not assume, however, that newer interpretations are always better; some older works have contributed significantly to the field and may offer interpretations that are still influential. (As you become more experienced in historical research, you will be able to determine which older sources are still useful.) Moreover, older sources might offer a historical perspective on how interpretations of an issue or event have changed over time.

DOES THE AUTHOR PROVIDE SUFFICIENT AND LOGICAL SUPPORT FOR HIS OR HER THESIS? Any book or article makes an argument in support of a thesis. (For detailed information on what a thesis is and a discussion of how the thesis relates to the argument of a paper, see p. 44). Once you have identified the thesis, you should evaluate the evidence the author uses to support it. You may not be in a position to judge the accuracy of the evidence, although you will build expertise as you continue to read about the subject. You can, however, evaluate the way in which the author uses the evidence he or she presents. You might ask yourself whether the evidence logically supports the author's point. For example, the eighteenth-century French philosophe Denis Diderot advocated religious tolerance, but this fact does not justify an assertion that all eighteenth-century Frenchmen were tolerant. Such an assertion would be a logical fallacy known as a *hasty generalization*.

You should also ask whether the same facts could be interpreted in another way to support a different thesis. For example, G. Stanley Hall, an early twentieth-century American psychologist, amassed evidence that demonstrated a correlation between a woman's educational level and the number of children she had: Women who attended colleges and universities had fewer children than their less educated sisters. From these facts, he concluded that higher education caused sterility in women. A modern historian looking at the same evidence might conclude that education allowed women to become economically independent, freed them from the necessity of forming early marriages, and allowed them to pursue careers other than raising children.

Another consideration is whether the cause-and-effect relationships described in a source are legitimate. It may be true that event A happened before event B, but that does not necessarily mean that A caused B. For example, an extremely bright comet was visible all over Europe in the autumn of 1066. That winter, Duke William of Normandy conquered England. We should not necessarily assume, however, that the comet caused the Norman conquest. This would be a *post hoc* fallacy, from the Latin *post hoc, ergo propter hoc* (after this, therefore because of this).

In addition, you should consider how the author deals with any counterevidence. (See pp. 50–51 for a discussion of counterevidence.)

HOW DOES THE SOURCE COMPARE WITH OTHERS I HAVE CONSULTED? Does the source add to your knowledge of the subject? How is it different from other sources you have read? Does the author contradict or disagree with others who have written on the subject? If so, which arguments or interpretations do you find most convincing?

2b-3. Evaluating Internet sources

Internet sites are often maintained by universities, museums, government agencies, and other institutions and can be a gold mine for students whose access to large research libraries is limited. Making effective use of this research tool, however, requires you to anticipate and avoid the special problems that it presents. The most significant difficulty that students encounter when trying to evaluate an Internet source is that although articles in scholarly journals and books from academic presses are carefully reviewed by other scholars in the field (and, in fact, may be available on the Web), anyone with the right software can post information on the Internet. Students should therefore be especially careful to determine the reliability of their Internet sources.

In attempting to evaluate an Internet source, students should first determine whether the source they are using is primary or secondary and ask the same questions they would use to evaluate a similar source in print. In addition, Internet users should consider the following:

- Is the author's identity clear, and, if so, what are his or her academic credentials? Does the author list an academic degree? Is he or she affiliated with a college or university?
- Does the author of the Web site provide evidence for his or her assertions, and does the site include source citations, bibliographies, and so on?
- Is the Web site affiliated with an academic institution, press, or journal? The Web address — or URL (uniform resource locator) — can provide some clues to such affiliations. If ".edu" or ".gov" appear in the address, it has been posted by an educational or governmental institution, which may give you some confidence in the material it contains.
- Is the Web site sponsored by a particular group or organization? (Look for ".org" in the URL.) Do you know anything about the interests and concerns of the person or group that publishes the Web site?
- Does the information on the Web site coincide with what you have learned about the subject from other sources?
- Has the Web site been updated recently?
- Does the Web site contain useful links to other sites? Are the linked sites affiliated with reputable institutions or persons?

If you are still unsure if the source is reliable, it is best to consult your professor or a reference librarian.

2c. Writing history papers

Aside from research papers, which will be discussed in a separate section, the most common writing assignments you will encounter are summaries, book reviews, annotated bibliographies, short essays, and historiographic essays. Each requires a slightly different approach.

2c-1. Summaries

Your professor might ask you to summarize a document, an article, or a section of a book. Because summarizing requires you to condense what you have read and put the author's ideas *into your own words*, it helps ensure that you have understood and digested the material. A summary (sometimes called a *précis*) should describe the author's main point, or thesis, and key evidence used to support it. A summary, then, essentially reports the content of the text; it should not include your critical analysis of the text. (See p. 40 for further advice on writing summaries.)

2c-2. Book reviews

A book review is not the same thing as a book report, which simply summarizes the content of a book. When writing a book review, you not only report on the content of the book but also assess its strengths and weaknesses. Students sometimes feel unqualified to write a book review; after all, the author of the book is a professional historian. However, even if you cannot write from the same level of experience and knowledge as the author, you *can* write an effective review if you understand what the assignment requires.

In writing a review you do not relate only whether you liked the book; you also tell your readers *why* you liked or disliked it. It is not enough to say, "This book is interesting"; you need to explain *why* it is interesting. Similarly, it is not enough to report that you disliked a book; you must explain your reaction. Did you find the book unconvincing because the author did not supply enough evidence to support his or her assertions? Or did you disagree with the book's underlying assumptions? Incidentally, when you are writing your review, it is unnecessary to preface statements with *I think* or *in my opinion* since readers assume that as a reviewer you are expressing your own opinions.

To understand your own reaction to the book, you need to read it carefully and critically. As a critical reader, you are not passive; you should ask questions of the book and note reactions as you read. Your book review then discusses those questions and reactions. (See pp. 13–20 for advice on critical reading.) Though there is no one correct way to structure a review, the following is a possible approach:

- Summarize the book and relate the author's main point, or thesis. (Somewhere early in the paper, identify the author briefly.)
- Describe the author's viewpoint and purpose for writing; note any aspects of the author's background that are important for understanding the book.

- Note the most important evidence the author presents to support his or her thesis.
- Evaluate the author's use of evidence, and describe how he or she deals with counterevidence. (See pp. 50–51 for a discussion of counterevidence.) Is the book's argument convincing?
- Compare this book with other books or articles you have read on the same subject.
- Conclude with a final evaluation of the book. You might discuss who would find this book useful and why.

NOTE: *Critical* does not mean negative. If a book is well written and presents an original thesis supported by convincing evidence, say so. A good book review does not have to be negative; it does have to be fair and analytical.

2c-3. Annotated bibliographies

A bibliography is a listing of books on a particular topic, usually arranged alphabetically by authors' last names. (See pp. 65 and 84–93 for further information on bibliographies.) In addition to providing bibliographic information, an annotated bibliography briefly summarizes each book or article and assesses its value for the topic under discussion. In writing your entries for an annotated bibliography, keep in mind the same questions you would ask while writing a book review. Remember that entries in an annotated bibliography should be relatively short; you will not be able to write a full analysis of a book or article.

Following is an example of an annotated bibliography entry:

Duus, Peter, ed. *The Japanese Discovery of America: A Brief History with Documents.* Boston: Bedford Books, 1997.

This book explores the relationship between Japan and the United States in the mid-nineteenth century, focusing on the dramatic differences between the two cultures and the uneasiness, confusion, and misunderstandings that arose from those differences. In a short introductory history, Duus discusses Japanese isolationism, the military and economic factors that led the United States to forcefully open relations with Japan, and the ways in which the Japanese observed and interpreted Americans and their culture. The main body of the text comprises a series of documents, including political pamphlets, autobiographies, eyewitness accounts, broadsheets, and prints. The inclusion of both Japanese and American views of Japan invites a comparison of mutual misunderstandings.

2c-4. History papers: General approaches

History students are most often asked to write two types of papers: short essays and research papers. Although these papers are different in some respects, they require similar approaches.

History papers usually include a narrative that recounts "what happened." Narrative is a basic element of history writing, and it is crucial that your account of past events is accurate. Nevertheless, a series of factual statements about the past, however precise they may be, does not constitute a history paper. You will not have written a history paper if you report that something (for example, the Manchu invasion of China, the death of the Aztec king Montezuma, the rise of Islam) happened. Rather, a history paper explores *how* and *why* something happened and explains its significance.

A history paper, like many other kinds of academic writing, usually takes the form of an *argument* in support of a *thesis*. A thesis is *not* a description of the topic, a statement of fact, a question, or an opinion, although it is sometimes confused with all of these things. Rather, a thesis is a statement that reflects what the author has concluded about the topic under consideration in the paper, based on a critical analysis of the source materials he or she has examined. A thesis informs the reader about the *conclusions* the author has reached. Moreover, a thesis is always an arguable or debatable point. In fact, the purpose of a history paper is to present the reader with enough evidence to convince him or her that the author's thesis is correct. As a result, the thesis is the central point to which all the information in the paper relates. As Edward Proffitt, author of *The Organized Writer,* puts it, "A paper is about its thesis and nothing else."[2] (For more on writing a thesis, see p. 46.)

In essence, then, when you write a paper in history, you are expected to interpret sources and, using those interpretations, to come to a conclusion about the meaning and significance of your subject. You express this conclusion in the main point, or thesis, of your paper. To support your thesis, you offer evidence from your sources. You should also respond to counterevidence, information that seems to contradict or weaken your thesis. (See pp. 44–47 for a discussion of the thesis and pp. 50–51 for a discussion of counterevidence.)

2. Edward Proffitt, *The Organized Writer: A Brief Rhetoric* (Mountain View, Calif.: Mayfield Publishing Company, 1992), 18.

Finally, you should remember that professional historians, working from the same sources, often form very different opinions about them. Thus it is unlikely that there is one correct interpretation of any topic that you will write about. You do, however, need to convince readers that your interpretation is a valid one. You will be able to do this only if you have provided *concrete evidence* — based on reliable sources — that supports your thesis and have responded honestly to opposing positions.

2c-5. Short essays

Unlike most research papers, essays are relatively brief (about five to ten pages), and the topic and text(s) are usually assigned. You might be asked, for example, to analyze a source or group of sources and respond to a specific question about them. Here is an example of a short essay assignment for a class in the history of science:

> Compare the views expressed by Nicole Oresme [a late-medieval natural philosopher] and Galileo Galilei on the role of religious beliefs in the study of the natural world.

In a different class, you might be asked to write an in-depth analysis of one text or to compare the views of two modern historians on the same issue. However different these assignments may appear to be, they all require similar responses.

ANALYZE THE ASSIGNMENT CAREFULLY. What will you need to know to write this paper? Make sure you identify and understand *all* the parts of the assignment. For the history of science example, it would not be sufficient to write a paper about Galileo using a few references to Oresme for comparison. You would need to understand what *both* Oresme and Galileo thought about the role of religious beliefs in the study of the natural world and give approximately equal weight to each in your discussion. Because the assignment asks you to compare the views of Oresme and Galileo, you would also need to understand both how their views are similar and how they differ.

You should also be careful to write about the topic that has actually been assigned. In reading Oresme and Galileo, for example, you may discover that both discuss the extent to which a natural philosopher should rely on the authority of Aristotle. Although this is an interesting issue, it is not the subject of the assignment.

CONSIDER THE SIGNIFICANCE OF THE MATERIAL. It is not enough to present a laundry list of similarities and differences or to report the contents of the texts you have read. Nor should your paper be composed of two minipapers — one on Oresme and one on Galileo — glued together. Instead, when you write a history paper, you are expected to consider the significance of the issue you are examining. In the sample assignment, the instructor's expectation is that the student will examine not only the ways the two authors are similar and different but the *meaning* of those similarities and differences. In responding to the sample assignment, you might discover, for example, that both Oresme and Galileo believe that God is the creator of the universe and the author of the natural laws that govern it. In writing the essay, you would be expected to discuss why this similarity is important. Or a comparison of the two texts might reveal that Oresme believes that the Bible can answer questions about the natural world, while Galileo argues that Scripture has no place in scientific discussions. In that case you should discuss the significance of this difference.

You should also think about the historical issue underlying the assignment. In this essay assignment, the student is asked to compare the views of Oresme, a fourteenth-century natural philosopher, with those of Galileo, who, two centuries after Oresme, became a central figure in the scientific revolution. One purpose of this assignment might be to encourage the student to think about the relationship between medieval and early modern views of the world.

CONSTRUCT AN ARGUMENT IN SUPPORT OF A THESIS. A short essay, like any paper in history, should have a thesis that is supported by evidence presented in the body of the essay. As noted earlier, your thesis reflects what you have concluded about the issue after careful reflection on the assignment and any reading that you have done for it. (See pp. 44–47 for further discussion of the thesis.) The student who concludes that Oresme's and Galileo's ideas are similar would write a thesis about the significance of those similarities:

> Popular descriptons of Galileo imply that he believed science and religion to be incompatible, but a comparison of his ideas with those of Nicole Oresme suggests that

Galileo's ideas about God and nature were similar to the
beliefs held by medieval natural philosophers.

The student who concludes that the differences
between Oresme and Galileo are more significant than
their similarities would write a thesis reflecting such an
interpretation:

Both Galileo and Oresme believe in God, but the similarity
ends there: While Oresme sees Scripture as the ultimate
font of all knowledge, Galileo dismisses it as irrelevant to
the issues explored by scientists.

Note that the writers of these two theses have read
the same texts and arrived at opposite conclusions,
neither of which is right or wrong. What is essential
is that the students be able to support their theses
with evidence taken from the texts. It is *not* enough
simply to make an assertion and expect readers to
agree.

RESPOND TO COUNTEREVIDENCE. Acknowledging
counterevidence — information that does not support
your argument — will *not* weaken your paper. On the
contrary, if you address counterevidence effectively, you
strengthen your argument by showing why it is
legitimate despite information that seems to contradict
it. If, for example, you wish to argue for continuity
between medieval and Renaissance science, you would
need to show that the similarities between Galileo's and
Oresme's ideas are more significant than the differences.
If you want to argue in support of the differences
between the two, you might try to show that their
similarities are superficial and that Galileo's rejection
of Scripture as a source of knowledge about the natural
world constitutes a significant change in the way people
thought about science. In either case, your argument
must be based on evidence and counterevidence
contained in the relevant texts, not merely on your own
gut feelings. (See pp. 50–51 for further discussion of
counterevidence.)

DOCUMENT YOUR PAPER. Even a short essay requires
that you cite and document the sources of your
information. (See pp. 61–65 for a discussion of when
to cite sources. Models for how to document various
kinds of historical sources can be found beginning
on p. 69.)

2c-6. Historiographic essays

Historians frequently disagree about how to interpret the events they study. For example, some historians have interpreted the Magna Carta, a charter signed by King John of England in 1215, as a revolutionary declaration of fundamental individual freedoms; others have seen it as a conservative restatement of feudal privilege. Similarly, historians interested in the same historical event might examine different sets of sources to answer the same question. In studying the causes of the French Revolution, Marxist historians might focus on economic and class issues while intellectual historians might concentrate on the impact of the writings of the philosophes (a group of French Enlightenment writers) on political thought and practice. To make students aware of debates among scholars and to acquaint them with a variety of inter-pretations, some instructors ask their students to write historiographic essays.

A historiographic essay is one in which you, acting as a historian, study the work of other historians. When you write a historiographic essay, you identify, compare, and evaluate the viewpoints of two or more historians writing on the same subject. Such an essay can take several forms. You might be asked, for example, to study the work of historians who lived during or near the time in which a particular event happened — for example, to explore the ways in which contemporary Chinese historians wrote about the Boxer Rebellion. A different kind of historio-graphic essay might require that you look at the ways in which historians have treated the same topic over time. For example, to examine how historians have treated Richard III, you might begin with the account of Sir Thomas More and end with the most recent study of Richard's reign. Yet another such assignment might ask you to compare the views of historians from several historical "schools" on the same event. You might, for example, be asked to compare Whig and Progressive interpretations of the American Revolution or Marxist and feminist views of the French Revolution. But in any case, a historiographic essay focuses attention not on a historical event itself but rather on how historians have interpreted that event.

A historiographic essay combines some of the features of a book review with those of a short essay. You should begin by reading critically the texts containing historians' interpretations, keeping in mind the questions you would need to answer if you were going to write book reviews about them (see p. 21). You should not, however, treat the historiographic essay as two or three book reviews glued together. Rather, you should synthesize your material and construct an argument in support of a thesis. The following thesis is from a student's essay on historians' interpretation of the colonial period of African history:

> Historians have held dramatically different views about the importance of European colonial rule in Africa: Marxist historians, along with others who focus on economic issues, have tended to see the colonial period as an important turning point, while cultural historians have maintained that the impact of the West on the ancient cultural traditions of Africa was superficial.

In the rest of the paper, the student supports the thesis, using the guidelines set out for a short essay (see pp. 24–26).

2c-7. Revising and editing your paper

One of the biggest mistakes that students make with any writing assignment is to leave themselves too little time to revise and edit their work. Although some students take a rather perverse pride in their ability to write a passable paper the night before it is due, the resulting work is never of the highest caliber and usually bears the hallmarks of careless writing: sloppy mistakes in reasoning, awkward constructions, poor word choice, lack of clear organization, and, of course, spelling and grammar mistakes. To write an effective history paper, you *must* allow yourself time to revise your paper.

When you revise, you need to read your paper critically, as if it were someone else's work. (For advice on critical reading, see pp. 13–20.) You should read for logic and clarity. You should make sure that your evidence is sufficient and that it supports your thesis. You should also look for wordiness and awkward sentence structure, for repetition and cliché. You must be willing to rearrange the order of material, do additional research to support weak points in your argument, and even change your entire thesis, if necessary. Obviously, you need to allow plenty of time for this part of the writing process, which may involve several drafts of the paper.

GRAMMAR AND SPELL CHECKERS. Running the spell checker and grammar checker on your computer is *not* the same as revising your paper. You should, of course, use both of these tools if they are available to you. However, running the spell checker will not pick up incorrectly used homophones (for example, *their, there,* and *they're*) or other words spelled correctly but used incorrectly. Nor should you rely on your grammar checker to catch every mistake. Always edit and proofread the final copy of your paper carefully; your instructor will not look kindly on a paper that is full of typographical, grammatical, and spelling errors.

2d. Taking essay exams

The essays you write for an exam will necessarily be shorter than the papers you write for your course, but they should follow the same basic format. In other words, an exam essay should begin with a thesis, stated clearly in the first paragraph, followed by several paragraphs in which you provide evidence supporting your thesis, and end with a conclusion. The difficulty, of course, is that you will be writing *this* essay under pressure, in a limited period of time, and without the opportunity to check the accuracy of your data.

Here are some suggestions for preparing to write a successful essay on a history exam.

2d-1. Preparing for the exam

The best preparation for an exam does not begin the day, or even the week, before the exam but takes place throughout the semester. Careful reading of the texts and periodic review of your notes on a weekly basis will ensure that you have a firm grasp of the material come exam time.

Throughout the semester, you should do the following:

- Attend class regularly, and take good notes. It is not necessary to write down *everything* your professor says. When taking notes, you should listen for the professor's *main points* and note the evidence that he or she gives to support those points. (You will discover that your professor's lectures usually follow the same format as a good essay.) Follow the same suggestions for a discussion class; your classmates will often make important points about the material you are studying.

- Review your notes regularly, preferably after each class. If you review your notes while the class is fresh in your mind, it will be easier for you to notice places where the notes are unclear. Mark these places, and clarify confusing points as soon as possible, either by researching the issue yourself or by asking your professor.
- Refer to your syllabus throughout the semester. Many professors provide detailed syllabi that state the themes for each section of the course. Use this as a guide for your own studying and thinking about the course material.
- Take careful notes on the material you are reading for the course. Keep in mind that simply copying long sections from your texts is not very useful in ensuring that you have understood the material. It will be much more useful for you to take notes in the form of summaries (see pp. 20–21 for a fuller discussion).
- If one is not assigned for the course, consider keeping an academic journal. In your journal, record important points about the material you are reading, any questions you want to answer or issues you would like to raise, important ideas suggested by class discussions, and so on. You can use the journal to track your growing knowledge of the material you are studying.

2d-2. The week before the exam

- Review your notes, syllabus, and texts. Identify the most important themes and issues of the course, and assemble the evidence that clarifies those themes.
- Imagine that you are the professor faced with the task of setting the exam for this course. What questions would you ask? Framing your own exam questions and answering them can be a useful way of organizing your thoughts.

2d-3. Taking the exam

BEFORE YOU WRITE. *Do not begin to write right away.* This is probably the biggest mistake that students make in essay exams. Before you write, do the following:

- Read the exam carefully. Make sure you understand what each question is really asking. You will not gain points by scribbling down everything you know about the development of Chinese politics from the tenth through the fifteenth century when the question asks you to discuss the impact of the Mongol invasion in 1260.

- If you are offered a choice, make sure you answer the question you can answer best. This may not always be the one you are drawn to first. One great insight about the significance of the Treaty of Waitangi will not be enough to write a good essay about Maori-British relations in nineteenth-century New Zealand. Be sure that you can cite several pieces of evidence in support of your thesis.

- Take the time to organize your thoughts. Jot down a quick outline for your essay, stating the thesis and listing the evidence you will provide to support that thesis.

WRITING THE ESSAY. Once you are ready to write, your essay should follow the same format as any other history essay:

- Begin by stating your thesis. *Do not* waste time restating the question: Your professor knows what he or she asked.

- Cite the evidence that supports your thesis. If you are aware of any counterevidence, make sure you discuss it. (See pp. 50–51 for a discussion of counterevidence and how to deal with it.)

- Be sure you *stick to the point*. Do not go off on interesting tangents that are irrelevant to the question. Referring frequently to your outline will help you keep on track.

- Tie your essay together by stating your conclusions.

3
Writing a Research Paper

A research paper, like a short essay, usually takes the form of an argument with a thesis supported by evidence. It is different from a short essay, however, in several ways. A research paper is more substantial, usually at least fifteen pages and often much longer. More important, a research paper, as its name implies, requires that you supplement assigned readings for the course with information from the library and other sources.

Your instructor might assign a specific research topic, or the choice might be left entirely up to you. Most often, you will be given some choice within a general area. The syllabus for a course with a research paper might, for example, include a statement like this in its list of course requirements:

> Research paper on any topic covered in the course, chosen in consultation with me. Your paper should be 15–18 pages and is worth 40% of the final grade.

Students often find such assignments intimidating and may secretly yearn for an assigned subject; it often seems easier to write about a topic that holds no interest for you than to face the task of defining your own area of investigation. However, when you choose your own research topic, you are engaged in the practice of history at a much more sophisticated level. You are, in fact, doing the same work that a professional historian does: answering the questions *you yourself* have posed about a subject that you find compelling or problematic.

Consider the following advice before you begin a research project.

3a. Thinking about your topic

A research paper represents a significant investment of time and effort. Before you begin, therefore, you should think carefully not only about your interests but also about the feasibility of your proposed topic.

CHOOSE A SUBJECT THAT INTERESTS YOU. Start with the texts assigned for your class, and find a general area that appeals to you. As you begin, your subject can be relatively broad — for example, "slavery and the Civil War." You will not know what problems, issues, and questions exist within the larger framework of the broad topic until you familiarize yourself with the general subject.

CONSIDER THE AVAILABILITY OF SOURCES. In deciding on a topic, you should consider what sources are available to you in your own college or university library. For example, you might decide that it would be interesting to examine the views of artisans during the French Revolution, but if you cannot obtain enough sources of information on this subject, this will not be a workable topic.

If your own institution's holdings are limited, you may be able to supplement them by borrowing materials from nearby colleges and universities or from more distant sources through interlibrary loan. Don't overlook public libraries, especially in larger urban centers; many have surprisingly good holdings. And, of course, you may be able to get sources over the Internet (see p. 37 for more on using Internet sources). Nevertheless, it is certainly easier to begin with a topic for which your own library has a reasonable number of sources.

Similarly, you should consider whether the sources for the topic in which you are interested are written in a language that you can read fluently. In the example cited above, for example, you might find that your library has a large collection of sources on artisans in revolutionary France — in French. In this case, consider whether your command of the language is sufficient for the research you hope to pursue.

NARROW YOUR SUBJECT DOWN TO A WORKABLE TOPIC. Once you have begun to gather materials related to your area of interest, you will need to narrow your subject down to a workable topic. After all, you will not be able to write effectively on a broad topic like "slavery and the Civil War" within the length of a typical research paper.

Narrowing your topic to one that is feasible always begins with reading; however, simply reading everything you can find about slavery and the Civil War will *not* help you find a suitable research topic. Your reading must be active, not passive. In other words, you must be actively engaged in a dialogue with the texts you are reading, constantly asking questions that direct your reading.

A history paper usually begins with a question, and you can begin to narrow your broad subject by rephrasing your topic as a series of questions. What is it that you want to know about "slavery and the Civil War"? Are you interested in the role of abolitionists in the war? In the events and ideas that led up to the Emancipation Proclamation? In what slaves thought about the war? List those questions, and try to answer them as you read. As you begin to answer some of your initial questions, you will gain a deeper knowledge of your subject, and more detailed questions will arise: What role did freed slaves play in Union regiments? How were black soldiers treated by their white commanders? If you read actively in this way, you will discover which questions have been thoroughly discussed and which are less well studied. You will find the areas in which historians have reached consensus and questions that are still the subject of debate. Ultimately, you may even find an area where you feel you can say something both interesting and original. At this point in the process of narrowing your topic, you will be able to generate the thesis that will drive your research paper. (For a more detailed discussion of the thesis, see pp. 44–47.)

Finally, write as you read. Most scholars would agree that reading and writing are interactive processes. Writing will help you clarify your thoughts about what you are reading and provide direction for your research.

START YOUR RESEARCH EARLY. The day you receive the assignment is not too soon to begin your research. Anticipate problems in gathering your sources: Other people may have borrowed the books you need, or you may have to travel to other libraries to use their collections. If you are interested in a topic for which your own library has only limited sources, you might be able to borrow books from other colleges and universities on interlibrary loan. But to ensure that you get your books in time, you will need to make your request early.

3b. Conducting research

A great deal of the work you do in writing a research paper happens *before* you begin to write your first draft. This section deals with the research skills that you will need to master to make the most of the wealth of material available to you.

BEGIN BY CONSULTING YOUR PROFESSOR. Although a research paper may seem daunting to you, you should remember that your professor has had a great deal of experience in conducting research and writing papers and is intimately familiar with the research produced by other historians. Take advantage of this expertise by utilizing office hours, chat rooms, Web sites, and other forums for consulting your professor. He or she will be delighted by your interest and will be happy to point you in a number of potentially fruitful directions.

GENERATE A WORKING BIBLIOGRAPHY. The next step in beginning your research paper is to generate a working bibliography. You should start your search in the library. If your professor has suggested sources, make sure you consult them at the outset of your research. Invaluable and often overlooked resources are reference librarians, who can direct you to important journals, bibliographies, and other research tools. Reference librarians can also teach you how to search the online catalog by using keywords to find recent books and journal articles in your library's collection. If your library has a card catalog, be sure to check it as well; many college libraries are still in the process of computerizing their holdings, and you may overlook important sources if you rely solely on the online catalog. Once you have found some preliminary sources, you can use their notes and bibliographies as a guide for gathering additional material. You may also be able to use your library's computer to search the holdings of nearby affiliated libraries; and, of course, you can conduct an Internet search as well.

NOTE: Do not make generating a bibliography an end in itself. You still need to read the books and articles you have found. Your final bibliography should include only the materials you have read and found useful in writing your paper.

USE BOTH PRIMARY AND SECONDARY SOURCES. In a research paper, you will need to consult primary sources (letters, diaries, original documents, and so on) from the period you are studying. You will also want to consult secondary sources to become familiar with the ways in which other historians have interpreted this material. Do not confine your research to books; important recent research is often found in articles in scholarly journals. (See Appendix B for guidance in researching primary and secondary sources.) Your instructor will be able to direct you to additional sources. Librarians are also extremely helpful in tracking down both printed and Internet materials.

USE NONWRITTEN MATERIALS WHERE APPROPRIATE. Although much of the work you do in an undergraduate history course will center on the reading and interpretation of written sources, historians also use a wide variety of nonwritten sources in their work. The following may be useful to you in researching and writing your paper:

- *Maps* are especially useful when you are trying to explain geographical relationships, such as the movements of troops during a battle, the changes in the national boundaries of a particular area over time, and the growth of trade routes. Many excellent maps are available on the Internet.
- *Graphs* and *charts* are useful for illustrating statistical information, such as rates of marriage, births, or deaths and changes in per capita income over a particular period of time.
- *Photographs, cartoons,* and other illustrations can provide evidence that may support or contradict the written sources (such as the photograph of Dreyfus's degradation, included on p. 9), or they may provide a unique perspective on events. Once again, many Web sites include photographs and other visual images.
- *Diagrams,* such as a sketch of the west portal of Chartres cathedral or architectural plans illustrating the floor plan and elevation of the Empire State Building, can help the reader understand how parts are related to a larger whole.

If you consult nonwritten material in your research or use it in your paper, you must cite it and provide complete bibliographical information, just as you would for any written source.

3b-1. Conducting an Internet search

The Internet offers countless possibilities for research. Due to the rapid expansion of the Internet, the amount of material available to any individual student has multiplied exponentially. The availability of information on the Internet is not, however, without drawbacks. Virtually anyone with a computer, a modem, and the right software can create a Web site. As a result, many Web sites are useless for serious research. (For help with evaluating Internet sources, see pp. 19–20). Nonetheless, the Internet is a worthwhile tool for research. This section will introduce you to a few online research techniques that can make your Internet searches more effective.

When you look for information on the Internet, you will usually use either a *directory* or a *search engine*. Both of these tools are useful, but they are not the same and require different methods to be used effectively.

USING DIRECTORIES AND SEARCH ENGINES. A *directory* offers a list of categories with increasingly specialized subcategories. A typical directory, like Yahoo!, begins with a list of broad general categories that contains a number of subcategories. For instance, under the general category "Social Sciences" you will find the subcategory of "History." Clicking on "History," you are invited to search by "Region," "Subject," or "Time Period" or by a number of special subcategories, including "Archives," "Oral History," and "Psychohistory." As you click through the subsequent levels of the directory, the topics become more and more specific.

Some difficulties are associated with using directories. For example, if you go to the Yahoo! directory and click on the broad category "Arts and Humanities," you will not find "History." However, if you click on "Arts and Humanities" and then click on "Humanities," you *will* find "History" as a subcategory. In general, then, when you search using a directory, you should think creatively about the categories with which your topic might be associated. If you don't find your topic on the first try, go back and try a different category until you find what you are looking for. It may not be possible to find a category that matches your topic exactly. Instead, look for the category that *best* matches your topic.

A *search engine* works somewhat differently from a directory. From your Internet server, you can access several search engines such as Excite!, HotBot, AltaVista, Lycos, and Infoseek. To look for a topic using a search engine, you enter a word or group of words into the "Search" box and click on the appropriate command ("Search Now," "Go," "Submit," and so on). The search engine then searches its database and generates a list of sources that contain the word or words you searched for. A different type of search engine is a **metasearch engine** such as **MetaCrawler** and **InferenceFind.** These engines will run your search terms through several search engines at once (see Figure 3.1).

NOTE: Many search engines include an "advanced search" feature, which allows you to use the engine more effectively to find a specific topic. Since each search engine is different, you should refer to the instructions each one provides on how to conduct an advanced search.

The success of such a search depends heavily on two things: You must choose the correct word or words for

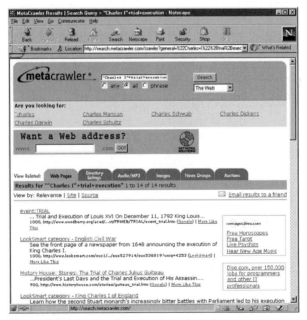

Figure 3.1   MetaCrawler, a metasearch engine

your search, and you must be willing to conduct several searches using alternative words (entering "Middle Ages" will turn up a different list than the one generated by entering "medieval"). Moreover, the search engine is not selective; it will list *every* source it finds, regardless of whether that source is relevant to your topic. For example, in writing a paper on the development of the papacy, you might search under "college of cardinals." Using a popular search engine, these keywords produced several promising sources — and also an article from the *Athens Daily Review* on the Trinity Valley Community College Cardinals football team of Athens, Texas. Second, you should never limit your search to one search engine. It is commonly assumed that search engines search the Internet: They *do not*. Rather, they search a *database*. Since each search engine uses a different database, it is essential to use several search engines for the best possible results.

Finally, the Internet provides a valuable research tool in the form of *hyperlinks* (or *links*). When you find a useful site, you will notice that some of the words for key ideas, people, and events appear in a color other than black or are underlined. These words indicate links. By clicking on a link, you can connect to other Web pages on the same subject. Thus, you can use links, just as you can use the notes and bibliography in a printed text, to find additional material. The presence of reputable, useful, and current links is also a good indication of the worthiness of a site. (For more on evaluating Internet sources, see pp. 19–20.)

NOTE: The results of an Internet search will probably contain many more irrelevant items than useful ones. While you are searching, it is therefore helpful to *bookmark* useful sites so that you can return to them for more careful study at a later date. Your bibliography must include complete bibliographical information about any Web sites you use. (For information on how to cite Web sites, see pp. 80 and 92.)

USE BOTH PRINT AND INTERNET SOURCES. The Internet has profoundly affected the ways in which students do research. Through the Internet, students in even the smallest colleges in the most isolated settings can access a wide variety of historical materials. However, it is important to remember that primary sources on the Internet are often not the best editions (see p. 17). Moreover, many primary and secondary sources are not yet available on the Internet. Students who rely solely on electronic media may miss many fundamental and indispensable sources. It is vital, therefore, that you consult both electronic and print sources in your research.

3c. Taking effective research notes

Your final paper will be only as good as the notes you take. There is no right or wrong way to take notes for a research paper. Many people favor 4" x 6" or 5" x 8" index cards, which can be arranged and rearranged easily. Others prefer to use notebooks or legal pads. If you have a laptop computer, you may wish to type your notes directly into an electronic file. This can be especially useful if you use a word processing program with a global search function so that you can use the search command to find keywords quickly wherever they appear in your notes. But whatever method you use, there are several things you can do to make your note taking more effective.

ALWAYS RECORD COMPLETE BIBLIOGRAPHIC INFOR-MATION FOR ANY SOURCE YOU CONSULT.   Nothing is more frustrating than to return all your books to the library, only to discover that you are missing authors' names, dates of publication, or other information you will need for your bibliography. (See p. 69 for a description of the elements that constitute "complete bibliographic information." If you have not written many academic papers, you may find it difficult to remember all of these elements; therefore, while doing your research, you may want to keep this guide handy. Or you may find it useful to list the information you need to record on an index card that you can carry with you.)

TAKE MOST OF YOUR NOTES IN THE FORM OF SUMMARIES. If you take notes word for word from your source, you are simply acting as a human photocopier. Your goal should be to digest the information presented in your sources and make it your own. It is therefore much more useful to read carefully and thoughtfully, close the book, and summarize in your own words the section you have read. Then compare your summary with the original, noting any important points that you missed or anything that you misunderstood. This type of note taking not only will ensure that you really understand the material but also will help you avoid plagiarism.

COPY QUOTATIONS ACCURATELY. If you do decide to quote directly from a source, make sure you copy the words and punctuation of your source exactly, and always use quotation marks so that you will know it is a direct quote when you return to your notes. Do not try to improve the wording of the original or correct the spelling or grammar. You may, however, alert your readers to an error in spelling or grammar by recording the error as it appears in the source and then noting the mistake by adding the Latin word *sic* in brackets, as follows: "Do not correct mispelled [sic] words."

DOCUMENT YOUR SOURCES. For a research paper, your professor will expect complete and accurate documentation of your sources. (See "Quoting and Documenting Sources," beginning on p. 57 for information on documentation.) Even if you are summarizing, you must note the source of your information and cite the source in your paper. Students sometimes assume, erroneously, that they need to document only direct quotations. In fact, "borrowing" ideas from other writers without documenting them is a form of plagiarism every bit as serious as stealing other writers' words. Any time that you use information derived from another person's work, adopt someone else's interpretation, or build on another writer's ideas, you must acknowledge your source. (See pp. 61–64 for a fuller discussion of avoiding plagiarism.)

AVOID THE MISCONCEPTION THAT "TO PHOTOCOPY IS TO KNOW." Photocopying material on your topic is no substitute for reading and understanding it. Photocopying doesn't save time; in fact, it's often a time waster. Eventually, you will have to read and interpret the photocopied material, and when you do, you may notice that you have copied irrelevant material and missed important information.

3d. Making an outline

The preliminary writing that you do for your research paper — listing questions, taking notes, jotting down ideas, and so on — is intended to stimulate and clarify your thinking and thereby help you narrow your initial broad interests into a workable paper topic. The result is the generation of a working thesis: a single sentence in which you state what you have concluded about your topic. (For a fuller discussion of the thesis, see pp. 44–47.) Once you know what argument you wish to make and have stated it in a working thesis, it is useful to sketch out the body of your paper in the form of an outline.

Some students have been trained to write formal outlines with roman numerals and various subheadings. If this method works for you, by all means use it. However, many students find formal outlines too constraining: One student said she can write such an outline only *after* her paper is written, which defeats its purpose.

The most important function of an outline is to provide a guide that notes the points you wish to cover and the order in which you plan to cover them. A good outline will help you present the evidence that supports your thesis as a convincing argument.

You might begin an informal outline by writing down the main points you want to discuss. These will form the topic sentences of paragraphs. Underneath each main point, list the evidence that supports it. Outlining your paper in this way will reveal any points that require additional evidence. It will also help ensure that your evidence is organized in a logical and orderly manner and that each idea is connected to those that precede and follow it.

NOTE: Remember that an outline is a *tool;* it is not divinely ordained or fixed in stone. As you continue to think and write about your subject, you may discover new material or change your mind about the significance of certain material. You may even change your thesis (which is why your thesis at this stage is a *working* thesis rather than a final one). When this happens, you must be willing to revise your outline too.

3e. Revising your research paper

A research paper is a complex project. You need to analyze your sources, synthesize information, organize your thoughts, and present them in a coherent and persuasive manner. As with a short essay, you must construct an argument with a thesis and supporting evidence, but in the case of a research paper, you will need to analyze and synthesize much more material. You will probably have more counterevidence to address as well. It is unrealistic to expect that one or two drafts will be sufficient to do justice to the project. Give yourself time to revise your writing.

4
Following Conventions of Writing in History

Each academic discipline has its own practices, or conventions, that people writing in the discipline follow when engaged in a scholarly dialogue. These conventions are not hard-and-fast rules, but following them will make it easier for you to participate in an academic conversation in your field. Moreover, many historians are excellent stylists. Your instructor will pay attention to your writing, so your attempts to learn and follow the conventions of the discipline will be noticed — and worth the effort. This section first looks at general conventions of writing history papers and then turns to concerns of word choice and grammar.

4a. Considering the whole paper

4a-1. Your relationship to your subject

When you write a history paper, you are not engaged in creative writing. Rather, you are forming a relationship of sorts with real people and events whose integrity must be respected. It is useful to keep in mind several conventions historians have established for such relationships.

RESPECT YOUR SUBJECT. The people who lived in the past were not necessarily more ignorant or cruel (or, conversely, more innocent or moral) than we are. It is condescending, for example, to suggest that any intelligent or insightful person was "ahead of his or her time" (suggesting, of course, that he or she thought the same way we do).

DO NOT GENERALIZE. Remember that groups are formed of individuals. Do not assume that everyone who lived in the past believed the same things or behaved the same way. Avoid broad generalizations, such as "the Middle Ages was an age of faith." At best, such statements are clichés. More often than not, they are also wrong.

AVOID ANACHRONISM. An anachronistic statement is one in which an idea, event, person, or thing is represented in a way that is not consistent with its proper historical time. For example, "Despite the fact that bubonic plague can be controlled with antibiotics, medieval physicians treated their patients with ineffective folk remedies." This sentence includes two anachronisms. First, although antibiotics are effective against bubonic plague, they had not yet been discovered in the fourteenth century; it is anachronistic to mention them in a discussion of the Middle Ages. Second, it is anachronistic to judge medieval medicine by modern standards. A more effective discussion of the medieval response to the bubonic plague would focus on fourteenth-century knowledge about health and disease, theories of contagion, and sanitation practices.

In short, you should not import the values, beliefs, and practices of the present into the past. Try to understand the people and events of the past in their own contexts.

BE AWARE OF YOUR OWN BIASES. We naturally choose to write about subjects that interest us. Historians should not, however, let their own concerns and biases direct the way they interpret the past. A student of early modern Europe, for example, might be dismayed by the legal, social, and economic limitations placed on women in that period. Reproaching sixteenth-century men for being "selfish and chauvinistic" might forcefully express such a student's sense of indignation about what appears to modern eyes as unjust, but it is not a useful approach for the historian, who tries to understand the viewpoints of people in the past in the social context of the period under study.

4a-2. The introduction and thesis

The introductory paragraph of your paper is in many ways the most important one and, therefore, the most difficult to write. In your introduction, you must (1) let your readers know what your paper is about, (2) put the topic of your paper into context, and (3) state your thesis — the position you are going to take on the topic. You must also attract your readers' attention and interest. The opening paragraph, then, has to frame the rest of the paper, and it has to make readers want to continue reading.

There is no magic formula for writing an effective first paragraph. You should, however, keep these conventions in mind.

DO NOT OPEN WITH A GLOBAL STATEMENT. Unsure of how to start, many students begin their papers with phrases like "Throughout history" or "From the beginning of time" or "People have always wondered about. . . . " You should avoid broad generalizations like these. First, you cannot prove that they are true: How do you know what people have always thought or done? Second, these statements are so broad that they are virtually meaningless; they offer no specific points or details to interest readers. Finally, such statements are so general that they give readers no clue about the subject of your paper. In general, it is much more effective to begin with material that is specific to your topic.

For example, the following opening sentence comes from a student's first draft of a paper on William Harvey, the seventeenth-century physician who discovered the circulation of blood:

> From ancient times, people have always been interested in the human body and how it works.

Although, strictly speaking, there is nothing wrong with this sentence, it is not a particularly effective opening. For one thing, it is such a general statement that readers will be inclined to ask, "So what?" In addition, it gives readers no indication of what the paper is about. Will the essay examine ancient Greek medical theory? Chinese acupuncture? Sex education in twentieth-century American schools?

In revising the sentence, the student eliminated the general statement altogether and began instead with a description of the intellectual context of Harvey's work:

> For the scholars and physicians of sixteenth-century Europe, observation and experimentation began to replace authoritative texts as the most important source of information about human anatomy and physiology.

From this short sentence, readers learn four things about the subject of the paper: the time frame of the discussion (the sixteenth century), the place (Europe), the people involved (scholars and physicians), and the topic (the relationship between authority and experience in the study of human physiology). Readers' curiosity is also piqued by the questions implied in the opening statement: Why did experimentation begin to replace authoritative texts? Was this change a subject of controversy? Who was involved? How did this change in method affect the science of biology and the practice of medicine? In other words, this opening sentence makes readers want to continue reading; they want to know the author's thesis.

INCLUDE YOUR THESIS IN THE FIRST PARAGRAPH. If your opening sentence has been effective, it will make your readers want to know the main point of your paper, which you will state in the *thesis*. The introduction to a journal article or book may be long, even several paragraphs, and the author's thesis may appear anywhere within it. Until you become skilled in writing about history, however, it is best to keep your introduction short and to state your thesis in the first paragraph.

Your thesis must be more than a description of your topic or a statement of fact; it should inform readers of your interpretation of the materials you have read and the conclusions you have reached. (For additional information on the thesis, see p. 23.) The following is the first draft of a thesis statement from a student paper on Samuel George Morton, a nineteenth-century physician and scientist who wrote several influential treatises on craniometry, the nineteenth-century science of measuring the human skull:

> Morton measured the size and shape of human skulls from various racial and ethnic groups, concluding that Caucasians had the largest skulls and were therefore superior to all other races.

This is not really a thesis at all. While it is an accurate description of what Morton did, it does not tell readers anything they couldn't learn from the most cursory reading of one of Morton's books.

Now look at the revised version of the thesis:

> Morton and his contemporaries used his skull studies, which he said were objective and quantitative, to justify their belief in the superiority of the Caucasian race; however, a close examination of Morton's work reveals, as Stephen Jay Gould has suggested, that his supposedly

scientific data were created by his own prejudices and racism.

This version of the thesis provides more than a simple description of what Morton did or said. Having studied Morton's works thoroughly and carefully, the writer has now come to a conclusion: Despite appearances to the contrary, Morton's studies were not scientific, and his data-collecting procedures were biased by his prejudices. Moreover, this thesis also tells readers why the writer thinks his topic is historically significant: Morton's views are important because they provided his contemporaries with a seemingly scientific justification for racism. Finally, this thesis statement anticipates the type of argument that will follow: The paper examines Morton's skull studies, discusses the ways in which they appear to be scientific, demonstrates the ways in which they are not scientific, and reveals the hidden biases and assumptions behind them. For all of these reasons, the revised thesis is much more effective than the draft thesis.

PLAN TO REWRITE YOUR OPENING PARAGRAPH. If you are having trouble beginning your paper, write a rough, temporary opening paragraph, and return to it when you finish your first draft of the entire paper. The act of writing your draft will help you clarify your ideas, your topic, and your argument. It may also help solidify your thesis and your opening.

4a-3. The body

In your introduction, you present your subject and state your thesis. In subsequent paragraphs, you provide evidence for your thesis and answer any objections that could be made to it. The following advice will help you to write well-organized paragraphs and make your argument clear and convincing.

BEGIN EACH PARAGRAPH WITH A TOPIC SENTENCE. Each paragraph should have one driving idea, which is usually asserted in the first sentence, or *topic sentence*. If you have made an outline, your topic sentences will be drawn from the list you made of the main points you wish to cover in your paper. (For advice on making an outline, see p. 41.)

MAKE CLEAR CONNECTIONS BETWEEN IDEAS. Each body paragraph provides evidence for your thesis in the form of examples, statistics, and so on. To be convincing, however, your evidence must be clear and well organized. Transitional words and phrases tell your readers how the individual statements in your paragraph are connected. To choose transitions that are appropriate, you will need to consider how your ideas are related to each other. Here are some transitional words or phrases that you might use to indicate particular kinds of relationships:

- **To compare:** *also, similarly, likewise*
- **To contrast:** *on the other hand, although, nevertheless, despite, on the contrary, still, yet, regardless, nonetheless, notwithstanding, whereas, however, in spite of*
- **To add or intensify:** *also, in addition, moreover, furthermore, too, besides, and*
- **To show sequence:** *first* (and any other numerical adjectives), *last, next, finally, subsequently, later, ultimately*
- **To indicate an example:** *for example, for instance, specifically*
- **To indicate cause-and-effect relationships:** *consequently, as a result, because, accordingly, thus, since, therefore, so*

DO NOT WANDER OFF THE SUBJECT. If you include a lot of irrelevant information, you will lose momentum, and your readers will lose the thread of your argument. Be ruthless: Eliminate all extraneous material from the final draft of your paper, however interesting it may be. For instance, if you are writing about the role that Chinese laborers played in the westward expansion of the American railroads, do not spend three paragraphs discussing the construction of the steam locomotive. If your paper concerns the American government's treatment of Japanese citizens during World War II, do not digress into a discussion of naval tactics in the Pacific theater. Similarly, you should avoid repetition and wordy sentences.

WRITING PARAGRAPHS: AN EXAMPLE. Here is a paragraph from the first draft of a paper on Chinese relationships with foreigners during the Ming period:

> The Chinese were willing to trade with barbarians. They distrusted foreigners. Jesuit missionaries were able to establish contacts in China. During the seventeenth

century, they acquired the patronage of important officials. They were the emperor's advisers. Chinese women bound their feet, a practice that many Europeans disliked. Relations between China and Europe deteriorated in the eighteenth century. The Jesuits were willing to accommodate themselves to Chinese culture. Chinese culture was of great interest to the scholars of Enlightenment Europe. Matteo Ricci learned about Chinese culture and became fluent in Mandarin. He adopted the robes of a Chinese scholar. He thought that Christianity was compatible with Confucianism. The Jesuit missionaries had scientific knowledge. In the eighteenth century, the papacy forbade Chinese Christians to engage in any form of ancestor worship.

This paragraph is very confusing. In the first place, it has no clear topic sentence; readers have to guess what the writer's main point is. This confusion is compounded by unclear connections between ideas; the paragraph lacks transitional words or phrases that alert readers to the connections that the writer sees between ideas or events. The paragraph is also poorly organized; the writer seems to move at random from topic to topic.

Here is a revised version of the same paragraph:

<u>The Chinese of the Ming dynasty were deeply suspicious of foreigners;</u> *nevertheless,* <u>Jesuit missionaries were able to achieve positions of honor and trust in the imperial court,</u> *ultimately* <u>serving the emperor as scholars and advisers.</u> *At first* glance, this phenomenon seems baffling; upon closer consideration, *however,* it becomes clear that the Jesuits' success was due to their willingness to accommodate themselves to Chinese culture. *For example,* one of the most successful of the early Jesuit missionaries, Matteo Ricci, steeped himself in Chinese culture *and* became fluent in Mandarin. To win the respect of the nobles, he *also* adopted the robes of a Chinese scholar. *Moreover,* he emphasized the similarities between Christianity and Chinese traditions. *Because* of their willingness to adapt to Chinese culture, Jesuit missionaries were accepted by the imperial court until the eighteenth century. Difficulties arose, *however,* when the papacy forbade Chinese Christians to engage in many traditional customs, including any form of ancestor worship. *As a result* of the church's increasing unwillingness to allow such practices, relations between China and Europe deteriorated.

This paragraph has been improved in several ways. First, a topic sentence, which is underlined, has been added to the beginning. Readers no longer need to guess that this paragraph will address the apparent contrast between sixteenth-century Chinese suspicion of foreigners and the imperial court's acceptance of Jesuit missionaries.

Second, the author has clarified the connections between ideas by including transitional words and phrases. These transitions, which are italicized, illustrate several different kinds of relationships, including contrast, cause and effect, sequence, and so on, and allow readers to follow the writer's argument.

Third, the paragraph has been reorganized so that the relationships between events are clearer. For example, the revised paragraph states explicitly that relations between China and European missionaries deteriorated in the eighteenth century because the church became less accommodating to Chinese customs, a relationship obscured in the original paragraph by poor organization.

Finally, the writer has removed references to the practice of foot binding and to European interest in China during the Enlightenment. Both are interesting but irrelevant in a paragraph that deals with Chinese attitudes toward Europeans.

ANTICIPATE AND RESPOND TO COUNTEREVIDENCE AND COUNTERARGUMENTS. Historical issues are seldom clear-cut, and historians often disagree with each other. Effective papers acknowledge disagreement and differing view-points. If you discover information that does not support your thesis, do not suppress it. It is important to acknowledge *all* of your data. You should try to explain to your readers why your interpretation is valid, despite the existence of counterevidence, but do not imply that your interpretation is stronger than it is by eliminating data or falsifying your information.

A student writing about the French Revolution, for instance, might argue that the average Parisian worker became a revolutionary not as a result of reading the political arguments of the Enlightenment thinkers but rather from desperate economic need. But the student cannot ignore the fact that many Parisian workers had read such works and that Enlightenment thinkers were often quoted in the popular press. Rather, a successful paper would acknowledge these facts and attempt to show that economic need was a more important or more immediate catalyst for political action.

Remember, too, that it is important to treat opposing viewpoints with respect. It is perfectly legitimate to disagree with the interpretations of other historians. In disagreeing, however, you should never resort to name-calling or oversimplifying or otherwise distorting opposing points of view. It is important to understand opposing arguments and respond to them fairly.

4a-4. The conclusion

Your paper should not come to an abrupt halt, and yet you do not need to conclude by summarizing everything that you have said in the body of the text. It is usually best to end your paper with a paragraph that states the most important conclusions you have reached about your subject and the reasons you think those conclusions are significant. You should avoid introducing new ideas or information in the conclusion. If an idea or fact is important to your argument, you should introduce and discuss it earlier; if it is not, leave it out altogether.

4b. Considering word choice and grammar

It is essential that your writing follow the rules of formal English grammar. Historians are just as concerned as English professors with grammatical issues such as comma placement, subject-verb agreement, sentence fragments, misplaced modifiers, run-on sentences, and unclear antecedents. If you are using a computer, a grammar-check program will help you avoid some of these mistakes, but it is no substitute for learning the rules.

It is beyond the scope of this manual to cover the basic rules of grammar. Any good style guide or writing manual will offer plenty of advice for writing clear grammatical sentences. (See Appendix A for a list of guides.) The following major points are useful to keep in mind when you write in history.

4b-1. Word choice

The words that you choose to express yourself with are a reflection of your own style. Nevertheless, here are a few guidelines.

AVOID CONVERSATIONAL LANGUAGE, SLANG, AND JARGON. Because history papers are usually formal, you should use formal language rather than conversational language and slang. For example, although it is perfectly acceptable in conversational English to say that someone "was a major player" in an event, this expression is too informal for a history paper. In addition, slang often sounds anachronistic: Historians do not usually describe an aggressive individual as being "in your face"; people are "killed," not "bumped off." Words with double meanings should be used only in their conventional sense: Use *cool* and *hot* to refer to temperature and *radical* to describe something extreme or on the political left. *Awesome* should generally be reserved for awe-inspiring things like Gothic cathedrals. You should also avoid jargon, or specialized language, which can often obscure your meaning.

MAKE YOUR LANGUAGE AS CLEAR AND SIMPLE AS POSSIBLE. In an effort to sound sophisticated, students sometimes use a thesaurus to find a "more impressive" word. The danger of this approach is that the new word might not mean quite what you intended. In general, you should use the simplest word that makes your meaning clear. Do not use a four-syllable word when a single syllable will do. Do not use five words (such as *due to the influence of*) where you can use one (*because*).

AVOID BIASED LANGUAGE. Always take care to avoid words that are gender-biased or that have negative connotations for particular racial, ethnic, or religious groups. You should never use expressions that are clearly derogatory. In addition, you should be aware that many words that were once acceptable are now deemed inappropriate. For example, the use of masculine words or pronouns to refer to both men and women, once a common practice, is now considered sexist by many. Use *humankind* or *people* rather than *mankind,* and do not use a masculine pronoun to refer to people of both genders.

In an attempt to avoid sexist language, students sometimes find themselves making a grammatical error instead. For example, in trying to eliminate the masculine pronoun *his* in the sentence "Each individual reader should form *his* own opinion," a student may write, "Each individual reader should form *their* own opinion." The problem with this new version is that the pronoun *their* is plural, while the antecedent, the word *individual,* is singular. The first version of the sentence is undesirable because it sounds sexist, and the second is unacceptable because it is ungrammatical. A grammatically correct revision is "Individual readers should form their own opinions." In this sentence, the antecedent (*readers*) and the pronoun (*their*) are both plural.

It is also important to realize that you cannot always rely on the books you are reading to alert you to biased language. For example, the author of a fairly recent study of the origins of racism consistently refers to Asian people as "Orientals," a term that was not generally thought derogatory at the time of the book's publication. Since then, however, the word *Oriental* has come to be seen as having a Western bias and should therefore not be used. Another example is the term *Negro,* which once was a respectful term used to refer to people of African descent. Today, the preferred term is *black* or *African American.*

NOTE: You cannot correct the language of your sources. If you are quoting directly, you must use the exact wording of your source, including any racist or sexist language. If you are paraphrasing or summarizing a paragraph containing biased language, you might want to use nonbiased language when it doesn't distort the sense of the source. Otherwise, put biased terms in quotation marks to indicate to your readers that the words are your source's and not yours.

4b-2. Tense

The events that historians write about took place in the past; therefore, historians conventionally use the past tense. Students are sometimes tempted to use the historical present tense for dramatic effect or to make the scene they are describing come alive, as in this example from a student paper:

> The battle rages all around him, but the squire is brave and acquits himself well. He defends his lord fearlessly and kills two of the enemy. As the fighting ends, he kneels before his lord on the battlefield, the bodies of the dead and dying all around him. His lord draws his sword and taps it against the squire's shoulders. The squire has proven his worth, and this is his reward; he is now a knight.

This use of the present may be an effective device if you are writing fiction, but it is awkward in a history paper. First, readers might become confused about whether the events under discussion happened in the past or in the present, especially if the paper includes modern assessments of the issue. Second, use of the present makes it easy for the writer to fall prey to anachronism (see p. 44). Perhaps more important, writing in the present sounds artificial; in normal conversation, we talk about events that happened in the past in the past tense. The same approach is also best for writing.

The present tense is used, however, when discussing the contents of documents, artifacts, or works of art because these still exist in the present. Note, for example, the appropriate use of past and present tenses in the following description:

> Columbus sailed across an "ocean sea" far greater than he initially imagined. The admiral's *Journal* tells us what Columbus thought he would find: a shorter expanse of water, peppered with hundreds of hospitable islands.

The events of the past are referred to in the past tense (*sailed, imagined, thought*), and the contents of the *Journal* are referred to in the present (*tells*).

4b-3. Voice

In general, historians prefer the active rather than the passive voice. In the active voice, the subject of the sentence is also the actor:

> Duke William of Normandy conquered England in 1066.

> By the seventh century, the Chinese had invented gunpowder, which they used to make fireworks.

> Emperor Gia Long, with French military and naval support, united Vietnam in 1802.

In the passive voice, the subject of the sentence is not the actor but is acted on:

> England was conquered in 1066.

> The process for making gunpowder was known in the seventh century.

> Vietnam was united in 1802.

Several difficulties arise when you use the passive voice. Persistent use of the passive voice can make writing sound dull. More important, however, the passive voice can often obscure meaning and create unnecessary confusion. And as you can see from these examples, readers cannot always tell who the actor is. We are not told, for example, who conquered England or who invented gunpowder.

Use of the passive voice also allows writers to avoid the complexities of some historical issues. In the second example, for instance, moving from the passive to the active voice forces the writer to be more specific: The Chinese invented gunpowder, but they used it for making fireworks and not for firing weapons. Similarly, in the third example, use of the active voice makes the writer think about *who* united Vietnam in 1802, which leads to a consideration of the relationship between Emperor Gia Long and the French military in bringing about that unity.

In addition, using the passive voice in the expressions "it can be argued that" or "it has been argued that" is equivocal. The first expression suggests that the writer is unwilling to take responsibility for his or her arguments. If your evidence leads you to a certain conclusion, state it clearly. Using passive expressions like "it can be argued that" suggests that you are not really sure that your evidence is convincing. Similarly, the expression "it has been argued that" confuses readers: Who has made this argument? How many people and in what context? Readers must have this information to evaluate your argument. Moreover, use of this expression can result in plagiarism. If someone or several persons have argued a particular point, you should identify them in your text itself and in a citation.

This is not to say, however, that you should never use the passive voice. Here, for example, is a description of the Holocaust (verbs in the passive voice have been italicized):

> Hitler engaged in the systematic and ruthless murder of the Jewish people. In 1933, Jews *were forbidden* to hold public office; by 1935, they *were deprived* of citizenship. In all, over six million Jews *were killed* as part of Hitler's "final solution."

In this passage, the writer wants to draw readers' attention to the recipients of the action — the six million Jews killed in the Holocaust. The persons acted on are more important than the actor. The passive voice, which focuses attention on the victims, is therefore appropriate here.

The passive voice, then, can be effective, but it should be used only occasionally and for a specific reason.

4b-4. Use of the pronouns I, me, *and* you

Until recently, most professional historians used the pronouns *I, me,* and *you* sparingly, if at all. This convention has been changing, however, and these pronouns are beginning to appear more regularly in history books and journal articles. Although many instructors still prefer that students avoid personal pronouns whenever possible, an increasing number of professors find their use not only acceptable but actually preferable to more labored constructions like "this evidence leads one to conclude that." Since the conventions governing the use of personal pronouns are in flux, it is best to consult your instructor about his or her preferences.

5
Quoting and Documenting Sources

Any history paper you write reflects your careful reading and analysis of primary and secondary sources. This section offers general guidance in incorporating source material into your writing through paraphrase and quotation. It also explains the conventions historians use to cite and document sources and will help you avoid the serious offense of plagiarism.

5a. Using quotations

Quotations are an important part of writing in history. Quotations from primary sources provide evidence and support for your thesis. Quotations from secondary sources tell your readers that you are well informed about the current state of research on the issue that you are examining. However, some students go to extremes, producing papers that are little more than a series of quotations loosely strung together. No matter how interesting and accurate the quotations, such a paper is no substitute for your own analysis and discussion of sources. In general, you should minimize your use of quotations, and you should choose the quotations you do use with great care.

The following guidelines will help you to decide when to quote and how to use quotations effectively.

DO NOT QUOTE IF YOU CAN PARAPHRASE. Summarizing or paraphrasing in your own words is usually preferable to direct quotation; it demonstrates that you have digested the information from the source and made it your own. In particular, you should not quote directly if the quotation would provide only factual information. Look at this passage from Bede's *Ecclesiastical History,* followed by a paraphrase:

ORIGINAL PASSAGE

When our holy father Augustine, the beloved of God, died, his body was laid to rest at the entrance to the church of the holy Apostles Peter and Paul, since the church was not yet completed or consecrated. But as soon as it was dedicated, his body was brought inside and buried in the north porch with great honour.[1]

PARAPHRASE

According to Bede, St. Augustine's burial had to be delayed because the church of Sts. Peter and Paul was still under construction at the time of his death.

Because the original passage is merely factual and not especially striking, the paraphrase would be preferable in a student paper.

DO QUOTE IF THE WORDS OF THE ORIGINAL ARE ESPECIALLY MEMORABLE. You might want to quote directly when your source says something in a particularly striking way. Read the following passage from the "Letter to the Grand Duchess Christina," in which Galileo argues that scriptural passages that describe physical phenomena need not be interpreted literally since the Bible is not a scientific text:

Now if the Holy Spirit has purposely neglected to teach us propositions of this sort [i.e., physical propositions] as irrelevant to the highest goal (that is, our salvation), how can anyone affirm that it is obligatory to take sides on them, and that one belief is required by faith, while the other side is erroneous? Can an opinion be heretical and yet have no concern with the salvation of souls? . . . I would say here something that was heard from an ecclesiastic of the most eminent degree: "That the intention of the Holy Ghost is to teach us how one goes to heaven, not how heaven goes."[2]

1. Bede, *Ecclesiastical History of the English People,* trans. Leo Sherley Price, 1955; rev. ed. R. E. Latham (Harmondsworth, England: Penguin, 1990), 180.
2. Galileo Galilei, "Letter to Madame Christina of Lorraine, Grand Duchess of Tuscany," in *Discoveries and Opinions of Galileo,* trans. with introduction and notes by Stillman Drake (New York: Doubleday, 1957), 185–86.

The quotation from the "eminent ecclesiastic" is memorable because of the play on words, which could not be duplicated in a summary or paraphrase. Galileo, then, chose an effective quotation.

You might also wish to quote when the original words are important to readers' understanding of the author's intentions or feelings. In the following passage from Plato's *Apology,* Socrates is addressing the jurors who have just condemned him to death:

> This much I ask from you: [W]hen my sons grow up, avenge yourselves by causing them the same kind of grief that I caused you. . . . Reproach them as I reproach you, that they do not care for the right things and think they are worthy when they are not worthy of anything. If you do this, I shall have been justly treated by you, and my sons also.[3]

In this passage, the tone is as important as the content. It would be impossible to capture in a summary or paraphrase the irony of the original.

5a-1. Conventions for using quotations

When you quote, you must follow the conventions for using quotation marks and integrating quotations in the text of your paper. Keep in mind the following important points.

INDICATE WHERE YOUR QUOTATION BEGINS AND ENDS. If you quote a source, you should quote the source's words *exactly,* and you should enclose the material from your source in quotation marks. If your quotation is more than four typed lines, you should set the quotation off by indenting it; this is called a *block quotation.* Block quotations are *not* enclosed in quotation marks. Typically, long quotations are preceded by an introductory sentence followed by a colon. You should use block quotations sparingly, if at all. Frequent use of long quotations suggests that you have not really understood the material well enough to paraphrase (see p. 57). Moreover, a long quotation can be distracting and cause readers to lose the thread of your argument. You should therefore use a lengthy quotation only if you have a compelling reason to do so.

---

3. Plato, *Apology,* in *Five Dialogues,* trans. G. M. A. Grube (Indianapolis: Hackett, 1981), 44.

KEEP QUOTATIONS BRIEF. To keep quoted material to a minimum, you should condense quoted passages by using the ellipsis mark (three periods, with spaces between), which indicates that you have left out some of the original material. If you are leaving out material at the end of a sentence, the ellipsis should be followed by a period (i.e., there will be *four* periods). The preceding quotation from Plato's *Apology* contains an example of this method.

FRAME YOUR QUOTATION. Quotations from sources cannot simply be dropped into your paper. Even if a quotation is appropriate to a point you are making, you cannot assume that its significance is immediately obvious to your readers. You should always make it clear to your readers how the quotation you have chosen supports your argument. This example is from a student paper on Judge Benjamin Lindsey, the founder of the first juvenile court in the United States:

> Like most progressives, Lindsey was interested in social reform. "I found no 'problem of the children' that was not also the problem of their parents."[4]

It is not clear how the quotation from Lindsey illustrates the writer's statement that Lindsey was interested in social reform. Are readers meant to assume that Lindsey wanted to remove children from the homes of unfit parents? Provide government support for indigent parents? Encourage state-funded family counseling?

In the revised version, the student frames the quotation in a way that makes its significance clear:

> Noting that youthful offenders were often the product of criminal environments, Lindsey argued that even the most vigorous attempts to curb juvenile delinquency would fail until more sweeping social reforms eliminated the economic and social factors that led their parents to engage in illegal activities. Addressing the need to rehabilitate and reeducate adult criminals, he wrote: "I found no 'problem of the children' that was not also the problem of their parents." Thus, for Lindsey, the reform of the juvenile justice system was intrinsically linked to the reform of adult criminal courts.

In this revision, the significance of the quotation as it pertains to the writer's argument is clear. The writer's

---

4. Benjamin Barr Lindsey, *The Beast* (New York: Doubleday, 1910), 151.

analysis before and after the quotation puts Lindsey's words in context.

5b. Avoiding plagiarism

Plagiarism is a *very* serious academic offense. The penalties for plagiarism are usually severe, ranging from an automatic F in the course to temporary suspension or even permanent expulsion from the university. In some circumstances, plagiarism may even be a crime. Although some individuals deliberately copy lengthy passages or even purchase whole papers, most student plagiarism stems not from dishonest intent but from lack of understanding about what exactly constitutes plagiarism. Most unintentional plagiarism can be traced to three sources: uncertainty about how to paraphrase, confusion about when and how to cite sources, and carelessness in taking notes and downloading Internet materials.

5b-1. Paraphrasing to avoid plagiarism

Most students know that copying a passage word for word from a source is plagiarism. However, many are unsure about how to paraphrase. Consider, for example, this passage from a textbook and the student "paraphrase" that follows:

ORIGINAL PASSAGE

In the early twentieth century, most Latin American nations were characterized by two classes separated by a great gulf. At the top were a small group of European-descended white people, the *patrones* (landlords or patrons), who, along with foreign investors, owned the ranches, mines and plantations of each nation. Like the established families of most societies elsewhere in the world, the *patrones* monopolized the wealth, social prestige, education, and cultural attainments of their nations. Many of them aspired to the ideal of nobility, with high standards of personal morality and a parental concern for those who worked for them. Some *patrones* lived up to these ideals, but most, consciously or unconsciously, exploited their workers.[5]

5. Richard Goff, Walter Moss, Janice Terry, and Jiu-Hwa Upshur, *The Twentieth Century: A Brief Global History,* 4th ed. (New York: McGraw-Hill, 1994), 62.

UNACCEPTABLE PARAPHRASE

In the early part of this century most Latin American countries were typified by two classes separated by a large chasm. At the top were a small group of white people, descended from Europeans, called *patrones*. Along with foreign investors, the *patrones* owned the plantations, ranches, and mines of their countries. Like aristocrats all over the world, the *patrones* controlled the wealth, social status, education, and cultural achievements of their countries. Many of them had high standards of morality and were concerned for their workers, but most, consciously or unconsciously, abused their workers.

In this example, the writer's attempt at paraphrase results in plagiarism, *despite the fact* that the second text is not an exact copy of the original. The writer has used a thesaurus to find synonyms for several words — *characterized* has become *typified, gulf* has been replaced by *chasm,* and *achievements* has been substituted for *attainments.* In addition, several words or phrases in the original have been left out in the second version, and the word order has occasionally been rearranged. Nevertheless, these changes are merely editorial; the new paragraph is not significantly different from the original in either form or substance.

NOTE: This paragraph would be considered plagiarism *even if* the writer acknowledged the source of the material; it is simply too close to the original to be considered the work of the student.

In a genuine paraphrase, the writer has thought about what the source says and absorbed it. Once the writer understands the content of the source, he or she can restate it in an entirely original way that reflects his or her own wording and style. Consider, for example, this paraphrase:

PARAPHRASE

The society of Latin America at the beginning of this century was sharply divided into two groups: the vast majority of the population, made up of the workers, and a wealthy minority, the *patrones,* who were descended from white Europeans. Although the *patrones* represented a very small segment of the population, they controlled the lion's share of their countries' wealth and enjoyed most of the social and educational advantages. Like their counterparts in Europe, many *patrones* adopted an attitude of paternalistic benevolence toward those who worked for them. Even if their concern was genuine, however, the *patrones* clearly reaped the rewards of their workers' labor.

This paraphrase is more successful; the writer has assimilated the content of the source and expressed it in his own words.

You will save time if you paraphrase as you take notes. However, if you attempt to paraphrase with the original source open in front of you, you are courting disaster. To write a genuine paraphrase, you should close the book and rewrite in your own words what you have read. (For advice on taking notes in the form of summaries, see p. 40. A shorter example of paraphrasing can be found on p. 58.)

5b-2. Citing sources to avoid plagiarism

When you derive facts and ideas from other writers' work, you must cite the sources of your information. Most writers are aware that they must cite the sources of direct quotations, but you must also provide citations for *all* information derived from another source, even if you have summarized or paraphrased the information. You must also cite your sources when you use other writers' interpretations of a historical event or text. Citing sources enables your readers to distinguish between your ideas and those of others.

The only exception is that you do not need to provide citations for information that is common knowledge. For example, you might have learned from a particular book that the Civil War spanned the years 1861 to 1865, but you do not have to cite the book when you include this fact in your paper. You could have obtained the time span of the Civil War from any number of sources because it is common knowledge. The more you read about your subject, the easier it will be for you to distinguish common knowledge from information that needs a citation. When in doubt, it is better to be safe and cite the source.

5b-3. Downloading Internet sources carefully

As with any other source, information derived from the Internet must be properly paraphrased and cited. A particular danger arises, however, from the ease with which Internet material can be downloaded into your working text. Whenever you download material from the Internet, be sure to create *a separate document file* for that material.

Otherwise, Internet material may inadvertently become mixed up with your own writing. Moreover, you should keep in mind that Internet sites are more volatile than print sources. Material on many Internet sites is updated on a daily basis, and a site that you find early in your research may be gone by the time you write your final draft. Therefore, you should always record *complete* bibliographic information for each Internet source *as you use it.*

5c. Documenting sources

For all of the sources in your paper, including visual and other nonwritten materials, you must provide complete bibliographic information. This enables readers to look up your sources to evaluate your interpretation of them or to read more extensively from them.

5c-1. Footnotes or endnotes

Historians usually use footnotes or endnotes to document their sources. With this method, you place a raised number, called a *superscript,* at the end of the last word of a quotation, paraphrase, or summary. This number corresponds to a numbered note that provides bibliographic information about your source. Notes may be placed at the bottom of the page (footnotes) or at the end of the paper (endnotes). In either case, notes should be numbered consecutively from the beginning to the end of the paper.

The following example shows a source cited in the text of a paper and documented in a footnote or endnote:

TEXT

Spurlock notes that when mesmerism came to America in 1836, "it was a method of curing sickness — a scientific triumph over magic."[3]

NOTE

3. John C. Spurlock, *Free Love: Marriage and Middle-Class Radicalism in America, 1825–1860* (New York: New York University Press, 1988), 85.

You should ask your instructor if he or she has a preference for footnotes or endnotes. If the choice is left up to you, weigh the advantages and disadvantages of each form. Footnotes allow your readers to refer easily and quickly to the sources cited on a given page, but they can be distracting. Further, historians often use explanatory or discursive notes, which contain more than simple bibliographic information. If your paper has a large number of such footnotes in addition to bibliographic footnotes, the pages might look overwhelmed with notes. If you use endnotes, you do not need to worry about the length of your notes. However, endnotes are less accessible, requiring readers to turn to the end of the paper to refer to each note.

5c-2. Bibliography

Papers with footnotes or endnotes also have a bibliography — a list of all the sources cited in the paper, arranged alphabetically by authors' last names (or by title where there is no author). In a paper with endnotes, the bibliography always follows the last endnote page. (See p. 97 for a sample bibliography.)

NOTE: An alternative form of documentation that is commonly used in professional journals in the social sciences is the author-date system. The author's last name and the publication date of a cited source are included in parentheses in the text itself; complete bibliographic information appears in a reference list at the end of the text. This form of documentation is almost never used in history. The author-date system is generally not practical for documenting many of the primary sources historians use. Occasionally, a history professor may suggest the use of the author-date system for a book review or for a paper citing only one or two sources, but you should not use it unless you are specifically told to do so.

5c-3. Documenting online sources

The Internet is an increasingly important tool for historical research. Since it is a relatively new tool, however, the conventions for documenting online sources are not yet firmly established. Nevertheless, it is essential that you provide your reader with enough information to locate and examine the material you have obtained from the Internet.

One useful source of information for documenting electronic sources is *Online! A Reference Guide to Using Internet Sources* by Andrew Harnack and Eugene Kleppinger (New York: Bedford/St. Martin's, 2000). Documentation models for Internet and other electronic sources can also be found in this manual on pages 80–82 and 92–93.

5c-4. Documenting nonwritten materials

Maps, graphs, photographs, cartoons, and other non-written materials can be useful in a history paper. It is not enough, however, to add these materials to your paper without discussion or explanation. When they appear in the body of a paper, visual materials, like quotations, should be incorporated into the text. They should include a caption that identifies the material, and the text accompanying any visual materials should explain their significance and their relationship to the topic under discussion. If you group visual materials in an appendix, you will also need to supply captions that identify the materials and their sources. Of course, using maps, photographs, and other nonwritten materials without full citations constitutes plagiarism. Like any other source, nonwritten materials must be cited in the bibliography.

5d. Using quotations and documenting sources: An example

A well-written history paper incorporates and documents source material. In the following paragraph, the writer has further revised the paragraph shown on page 49 to include short quotations, block quotations, citations of both primary and secondary sources, and a discursive footnote:

> The Chinese of the Ming dynasty were generally "uninterested in, and at times hostile to, things foreign."[1] The comments of one Ming official, Chang Han, reflect the attitude of many of his contemporaries:
>
>> Foreigners are recalcitrant and their greed knows no bounds. . . . What is more, the greedy heart is unpredictable. If one day they break the treaties and invade our frontiers, who will be able to defend us against them?[2]

1. John K. Fairbank and Edwin O. Reischauer, *China: Tradition and Transformation,* rev. ed. (Boston: Houghton Mifflin, 1989), 179.
2. Chang Han, "Essay on Merchants," trans. Lily Hwa, in *Chinese Civilization and Society: A Sourcebook,* ed. Patricia Buckley Ebrey (New York: Free Press, 1981), 157.

Despite this distrust, Jesuit missionaries were able to achieve positions of honor and trust in the imperial court, ultimately serving the emperor as scholars and advisers. It seems clear that the Jesuits' success in establishing cordial relations with the Chinese court was due to their initial willingness to accommodate themselves to Chinese culture. For example, realizing the extent to which the Chinese distrusted foreigners, one of the most successful of the early Jesuit missionaries, Matteo Ricci, steeped himself in Chinese culture and became fluent in Mandarin. Recognizing the importance of converting the highly educated members of the court,[3] Ricci adopted the robes of a Chinese scholar.[4] Moreover, he emphasized the similarities between Christianity and Chinese tradition, presenting Christianity as "a system of wisdom and ethics compatible with Confucianism."[5] Because of their willingness to adapt to Chinese culture, Jesuit missionaries were accepted by the imperial court until the eighteenth century. Difficulties arose, however, when the papacy forbade Chinese Christians to engage in many traditional customs, including any form of ancestor worship.[6] As the church became less accommodating to Chinese culture, relations between China and Europe deteriorated.

3. For a discussion of important converts to Christianity among educated Chinese, see Jacques Gernet, *A History of Chinese Civilization*, trans. J. R. Foster and Charles Hartman, 2d ed. (Cambridge: Cambridge University Press, 1996), 456–58.

4. Gernet, 450.

5. Fairbank and Reischauer, 245.

6. Gernet, 519; Fairbank and Reischauer, 249.

Documentation Models for Footnotes or Endnotes

Source

5e. Documentation models: Notes and bibliographic entries

The following models of notes and bibliographic entries illustrate the types of sources commonly used in history. The models follow *The Chicago Manual of Style,* 14th ed. (Chicago: University of Chicago Press, 1993). Your professor will probably tell you which style guide to use. (Many instructors ask their students to use Kate L. Turabian's *A Manual for Writers,* which follows *The Chicago Manual of Style.*) Whatever style you use, be consistent: If your first footnote or endnote follows the *Chicago Manual* form, all of your notes and your bibliography must follow the *Chicago Manual.*

NOTE: Notes and bibliographies follow different forms. Models for notes are given on pages 69 to 82. Bibliographic entries for the same sources are given on pages 84 to 93.

Models for footnotes or endnotes

Books

A typical note for a book includes the following information:

- The author's full name (or the editor's full name, if no author is listed), followed by a comma;
- The full title of the book, underlined or italicized;
- Publication information: the city of publication, followed by a colon (no state is needed for well-known cities); the name of the publisher, followed by a comma ("Inc.," "Co.," and other abbreviations are not needed); and the date of publication — all enclosed in parentheses and followed by a comma;
- The page or pages cited, followed by a period.

Individual entries should be single-spaced; double-space between notes. Typically, the first line of each note is indented.

1. BASIC FORM FOR A BOOK

    1. Henry Mayer, <u>All on Fire: William Lloyd Garrison and the Abolition of Slavery</u> (New York: St. Martin's Press, 2000), 22-25.

2. SHORTENED FORMS IN SUBSEQUENT REFERENCES

The first time you cite a work, you must provide complete bibliographic information. In subsequent references, however, use a shortened form. There are two acceptable methods to shorten a reference. In one, you can cite the author's last name followed by a comma and the page or pages cited.

```
2. Mayer, 220.
```

In the second, you may also include a shortened form of the title in your subsequent reference. This is necessary if you cite more than one work by the same author in your paper or if a subsequent reference appears long after the first reference. To shorten the title, use the key word or words from the title of the book or article.

```
3. Mayer, Garrison and Abolition, 101.
```

3. ABBREVIATIONS IN SUBSEQUENT REFERENCES

Ibid.   The abbreviation "ibid." (from the Latin *ibidem,* meaning "in the same place") is sometimes used to refer to the work cited in the previous note. However, many professors and professional journals prefer the author/page or the author/short title/page style. Be sure you know which method your professor prefers.

When it is used, "ibid." stands in place of both the author's name and the title of the work. If you are referring to the same page, use "ibid." alone; if you are referring to different page numbers, use "ibid." followed by a comma and the new page numbers.

```
4. Ibid., 79-84.
```

NOTE: Never use "ibid." if the previous note refers to more than one work.

Idem   If you are citing several works by the same author within the same note, you can use the word "idem" (Latin for "the same") in place of the author's name after the first reference.

```
5. Samuel Brunk, Revolution and Betrayal: A
Life of Emiliano Zapata (Albuquerque: University
of New Mexico Press, 1995), 288; idem, "The Sad
Situation of Civilians and Soldiers: The Banditry
of Zapatismo in the Mexican Revolution," American
Historical Review 101 (1996): 342.
```

Op. cit. and loc. cit.   The *Chicago Manual* discourages the use of either "op. cit." (meaning "in the work cited") or "loc. cit." ("in the place cited") to refer to the title of a work cited earlier. Use one of the two shortened forms instead.

4. TWO OR MORE AUTHORS

If a book has two or more authors, list the authors in your note in the order in which their names appear on the title page.

> 6. James Bradley and Ron Powers, Flags of Our Fathers (New York: Bantam Books, 2000), 78-80.

NOTE: For books with more than three authors, you may use the Latin term "et al." ("and others") after the first author instead of listing all the authors (for example, "Jane Doe et al.").

5. AUTHOR'S NAME IN THE TITLE

Sometimes an author's name appears in the title of a book, as in an autobiography or a collection of letters or papers. In this case, your footnote or endnote should begin with the title of the book.

> 7. Charles Darwin's Letters: A Selection, 1825-1859, ed. Frederick Burkhardt (Cambridge: Cambridge University Press, 1996), 15-19.

6. ANONYMOUS WORK

If the author of a work is unknown and if there is no editor or compiler, begin your note with the title.

> 8. DK Atlas of World History (New York: Dorling Kindersley, 2000), 33.

7. EDITED OR COMPILED WORK WITHOUT AN AUTHOR

Cite a book by its editor (abbreviated "ed.") or compiler (abbreviated "comp.") if no author appears on the title page (as in a collection or anthology).

> 9. Gregory L. Freeze, ed., Russia: A History (New York: Oxford University Press, 2000), 65-66.

8. EDITED WORK WITH AN AUTHOR

If an author's name is provided in addition to an editor's, give the editor's name after the title.

    10. Efraim Karsh, Empires of the Sand: The
Struggle for Mastery in the Middle East, 1789-
1923, ed. Inari Karsh (Cambridge: Harvard
University Press, 1999), 303-304.

9. TRANSLATED WORK

A translator's name, like an editor's, is placed after
the title when an author's name is given. If a source
has an editor and a translator, then both should be
listed.

    11. Julia Tunon, Women in Mexico: A Past
Unveiled, trans. Alan Hynds (Austin: University
of Texas Press, 1999), 52-57.

    12. Roman Vishniac, Children of a Vanished
World, S. Mark Taper Foundation Book in Jewish
Studies, ed. Mara Vishniac Kohn, trans. Miriam
Hartman Flacks (Berkeley: University of
California Press, 1999), 23.

10. MULTIVOLUME WORK

You can cite matierial from a single volume in a
multivolume work in one of two ways. You can give the
name of the volume first:

    13. The Wartime Genesis of Free Labor: The
Upper South, ed. Ira Berlin, vol. 1 of Freedom: A
Documentary History of Emancipation, 1861-1867
(New York: Cambridge University Press, 1993),
321-23.

or you can give the series name first:

    14. Freedom: A Documentary History of
Emancipation, 1861-1867, vol. 1, The Wartime
Genesis of Free Labor: The Upper South, ed. Ira
Berlin (New York: Cambridge University Press,
1993), 321-23.

If an individual volume of a multivolume work does
not have its own title, include the volume number and
the page numbers after the publication information.

    15. Cambridge History of American Foreign
Relations (Cambridge: Cambridge University Press,
1993), 1:32-33.

11. ARTICLE IN A COLLECTION OR ANTHOLOGY

If you cite an article in a collection or anthology, include the author and title of the article, followed by the title, editor, and publication information for the book in which it appears. Also give the page or pages on which the information you are citing appears.

16. Karen Kilcup, "Nancy Ward and Early Cherokee Women," in <u>Native American Women's Writing</u> (Malden, Mass: Blackwell, 2000), 12.

12. LETTER IN A PUBLISHED COLLECTION

When citing a letter that appears in a published collection, list the sender, recipient, and date of the communication, and then cite the collection in the usual way.

17. An Expectant Mother to Eleanor Roosevelt, 2 January 1935, <u>America 1900-1999: Letters of the Century</u>, ed. Lisa Grunwald and Stephen J. Adler (New York: Dial Press, 1999), 223.

13. EDITION OTHER THAN THE FIRST

If the text you are using is not the first edition, provide the edition number in your note.

18. Chafe, William H., <u>The Unfinished Journey: America since World War II</u>, 4th ed. (New York: Oxford University Press, 1999), 247.

14. WORK IN A SERIES

Some books are part of a series: publications on the same general subject that are supervised by a general editor or group of editors. The series title and series editor may be eliminated from your note if the book can be located easily without them.

19. Robert H. Abzug, <u>America Views the Holocaust, 1933-1945</u>, Bedford Series in History and Culture, ed. Natalie Zemon Davis and Ernest R. May (Boston: Bedford/St. Martin's, 1999), 194-197.

Periodicals

A typical note for an article in a journal includes the following information:

- The author's full name, followed by a comma;
- The title of the article, in quotation marks and followed by a comma;
- The name of the journal in which the article appears, underlined or italicized;
- The volume number (in arabic numerals, even if the journal uses roman numerals);
- The date, in parentheses, followed by a colon;
- The page or pages cited, followed by a period.

15. ARTICLE IN A JOURNAL PAGINATED BY VOLUME

Most scholarly journals are paginated consecutively throughout the volume. When citing an article from such a journal, you do not need to give the issue number, although this information may be useful, especially for recent, unbound journals.

> 20. Ned C. Landsman, "Nation, Migration, and the Province in the First British Empire: Scotland and the Americas, 1600-1800," American Historical Review 104 (1999): 463.

16. ARTICLE IN A JOURNAL PAGINATED BY ISSUE

If a journal paginates each issue separately, you must provide the issue number. In the following model (one of several acceptable forms for citing the issue of a journal), the volume number is 283, the issue number is 5, the year of publication is 2000, and the page reference is 668.

> 21. Rhoda Wynn, "Saints and Sinners: Women and the Practice of Medicine throughout the Ages," Journal of the American Medical Association 283, no. 5 (2000): 668.

NOTE: If you wish to include the month of publication, put it before the year: (March 2000). If you include the month, you do not need the issue number.

17. ARTICLE IN A POPULAR MAGAZINE

In citing an article from a popular magazine, include the author, title of the article, magazine title, and date (not in parentheses). Omit the volume and issue numbers. It is not necessary to include page numbers; if you do include them, they should be preceded by a comma, not a colon.

22. Michael Elliott and Michael Hirsh, "Learning the Lessons of Kosovo," Newsweek Special Edition, December 1999-February 2000, 22-26.

18. NEWSPAPER ARTICLE

When referring to an article in a daily newspaper, always cite the author's name (if it is given), the title of the article, date, month, and year. Each issue of a newspaper may go through several editions, and in each edition articles may be rearranged or even eliminated entirely. For this reason, you should cite the name of the edition in which the article appeared (for example, first edition, late edition). Page numbers are usually omitted. If you are citing a large newspaper that is published in sections, include the name, letter, or number of the section.

23. Steve Penn, "A New Home for Black History Archives to Get More Room for Memorabilia," Kansas City Star, 4 February 2000, sec. B, final edition.

NOTE: If the city of the newspaper is not well known, include the state in parentheses.

19. BOOK REVIEW

To cite a book review, begin with the reviewer's name followed by the title of the review, if one is given. Follow this information by the words "review of," the title of the work being reviewed, and its author. Also cite the periodical in which the review appears and the relevant publication information. If the author of the review is not named, begin with the title of the review or, if the review is untitled, with the words "Review of."

24. Ilene Cooper, review of Nat Turner's Slave Rebellion in American History, by Judith Edwards, Booklist 96 (2000): 1093.

25. Review of A Middle East Mosaic: Fragments of Life, Letters and History, by Bernard Lewis, ed., Publishers Weekly, 24 March 2000, 80.

Public documents

In the United States, most federal government publications are printed by the Government Printing Office in Washington, D.C., and may be issued by both houses of Congress (the House of Representatives and the Senate); by the executive departments (for example, the Department of State, the Department of the Interior, and so on); or by government commissions or agencies (for example, the Securities and Exchange Commission). In addition, public documents may be issued by state or local governments. A reference to a public document should include the following:

- The name of the country, state, city, or county from which the document was issued (papers on United States history may omit "United States" or "U.S.");
- The name of the legislative body, court, executive department, or other agency issuing the document;
- The title of the document or collection, if given;
- The name of the author, editor, or compiler;
- The report number;
- The publisher, if applicable ("Government Printing Office" may be shortened to "GPO");
- The date;
- The page or pages cited.

The following models are for notes citing government documents commonly used by students writing history papers.

20. PRESIDENTIAL PAPERS

The Government Printing Office has published the papers of the presidents of the United States in two multivolume collections: *Compilation of the Messages and Papers of the Presidents, 1789–1897* for the early presidency and *Public Papers of the Presidents of the United States* for twentieth-century presidents.

```
        26. Dwight D. Eisenhower, Public Papers of
the Presidents of the United States: Dwight D.
Eisenhower, 1953 (Washington, D.C.: GPO, 1960),
228-30.
```

21. EXECUTIVE DEPARTMENT DOCUMENT

A note for a document issued by one of the executive departments begins with the issuing department. Include the name of the author of the document, if it is known. If the publication is part of a series, you may include the series number and omit the publication information.

27. U.S. General Accounting Office, <u>Desert Shield and Desert Storm Reports and Testimonies, 1991-93</u> (Washington, D.C.: General Accounting Office, 1994), 446.

28. U.S. Department of State, <u>Belarus</u>, Background Notes Series, no. 10344, 77.

22. TESTIMONY BEFORE A COMMITTEE

Transcripts of testimony presented before congressional committees or commissions can be found in records called "hearings." Begin the note with the committee or commission name.

29. House Committee on Veterans' Affairs, <u>Radiation Research in the VA Involving Human Subjects: Hearing before the Committee on Veterans' Affairs</u>, 103d Cong., 2d sess., 1994, 367.

23. CONGRESSIONAL COMMITTEE PRINT

Both houses of Congress issue research reports called "Committee Prints." Your note should include either the date or the Committee Print number, if one is provided.

30. U.S. Congress, Senate Committee on Foreign Relations, <u>Inter-American Foundation Projects in Argentina and Haiti: A Staff Report to the Committee on Foreign Relations</u>, 106th Cong., 2d sess., 2000, 110.

24. TREATY

Treaties can be found in volumes of *United States Treaties and Other International Agreements,* issued by the Government Printing Office. Each treaty in the bound volume was originally published in pamphlet form in a State Department series titled Treaties and Other International Acts (TIAS). In your note, the title (in quotation marks) and date of a treaty should follow the name of the issuing agency (such as U.S. Department of State). The number assigned to the treaty in TIAS is given in the bound volume and should also be included in your note.

31. U.S. Department of State, "Jay Treaty,"
19 November 1794, TIAS no. 105, United States
Treaties and Other International Agreements, vol.
2, 245.

25. UNITED STATES CONSTITUTION

The Constitution is cited by article (abbreviated "art.") or amendment ("amend.") and section ("sec.").

32. U.S. Constitution, art. 4, sec. 1.

The forms of notes for state and local government publications are essentially the same as those for federal government publications.

Other sources

26. UNPUBLISHED THESIS OR DISSERTATION

To cite an unpublished thesis or dissertation, give its author, title (in quotation marks), academic institution, and date.

33. Robert James Nemes, "Between Reform and
Revolution: Associations, Culture and Politics in
Budapest, 1800-1849" (Ph.D. diss., Columbia
University, 1999), 170.

27. ILLUSTRATION

In citing an illustration in a printed text, give both the page number on which the illustration appears and the figure or plate number, if one is provided.

34. Time/CBS News, People of the Century
(New York: Simon & Schuster, 1999), 159.

28. SOUND RECORDING

Notes for sound recordings, including audiotapes, compact discs, and records, begin with the composer's name followed by the title of the recording (underlined or italicized) and the name of the performer. Also provide the name of the recording company and the number.

35. Gustav Holst, The Planets, Royal
Philharmonic Orchestra, André Previn, Telarc
compact disc 80133.

For an anonymous work or a collection of works by several composers, begin with the title.

36. <u>Virtuoso Recorder Music</u>, Amsterdam Loeki
Stardust Quartet, Decca compact disc 414 277-2.

29. FILM OR VIDEOCASSETTE

A note for a film or videocassette should include the title of the episode (if part of a series), the title of the film, the name of the producer and director, the playing time, the name of the production company, and the date. Videocassettes should be identified as such.

37. "Forever Free," <u>The Civil War</u>, prod. Ken
Burns, 11 hours, PBS Video, 1990, videocassette.

30. INTERVIEW

A note for an interview that has been published or broadcast on radio or television should include the name of the person interviewed, the title of the interview (if any), the name of the person who conducted the interview, the medium in which the interview appeared (radio, television, book, journal), and the facts of publication.

38. Timothy McVeigh, interviewed by Ed
Bradley, <u>60 Minutes</u>, Columbia Broadcasting
System, 26 March 2000.

31. PERSONAL COMMUNICATION

A note for an interview you have conducted in person or by telephone should include the name of the person you interviewed, the words "interview by author," the place of the interview, if applicable, and the date of the interview.

39. Nico Milkov, telephone interview by
author, 2 October 1999.

A personal letter or memorandum to you should be cited in the same way as a personal interview.

40. Audrey Hamilton, letter to author, 15
March 1998.

32. REFERENCE WORK

In a note for a standard reference work that is arranged alphabetically, such as a dictionary or an encyclopedia, omit the publication information and the volume and page references. You must, however, note the edition if it is not the first. After the name and edition of the work,

use the abbreviation "s.v." (for *sub verbo,* "under the word")
followed by the title of the entry in quotation marks.

    41. Encyclopaedia Britannica, 15th ed., s.v.
"steam power."

    42. Merriam-Webster's Collegiate Dictionary,
10th ed., s.v. "civilization."

33. BIBLICAL REFERENCE

When referring to a passage from the Bible, cite the book
(abbreviated), chapter, and verse, either in the text or in a
note. Do not provide a page number. In your first biblical
reference, identify the version of the Bible you are using;
in subsequent references, abbreviate the version.

    43. Matt. 20.4-9 Revised Standard Version.

    44. 1 Chron. 4.13-15 RSV.

Chapters and verses in biblical references have
traditionally been separated by a colon, but in current
usage they are separated by a period.

34. INDIRECT SOURCE

If material you wish to use from a source has been taken
from another source, it is always preferable to find and
consult the original source. If this is not possible, you must
acknowledge both the original source of the material and
your own source for the information.

    45. George Harmon Knoles, The Jazz Age
Revisited: British Criticism of American
Civilization during the 1920s (Stanford: Stanford
University Press, 1955), 31, quoted in C. Vann
Woodward, The Old World's New World (Oxford:
Oxford University Press, 1991), 46.

Electronic sources

The following models are based on the guidelines found
in *Online! A Reference Guide to Using Internet Sources* by
Andrew Harnack and Eugene Kleppinger (Bedford/St.
Martin's, 2000).

35. WEB SITE

To cite a document that is available on the World Wide
Web, the following information should be included: the
author's name, if known; the title of the document, in

quotation marks; the title of the complete work, if applicable, in italics or underlined; the date of the publication or last revision (if not known, use "n.d."); the URL (uniform resource locator), in angle brackets; and the date of access, in parentheses.

> 46. A. Martin, "Napoleon Bonaparte," n.d., <http://www.napoleon1er.com> (22 March 2000).

36. GOPHER SITE

Include the author's name, if available; the title; the title of the complete work, if applicable; the version and date, if known; the gopher address; and the date of access.

> 47. P. J. Stahl, "Questions Concerning Oswald's Personality," <u>The Real FAQ: Questions Concerning Lee Harvey Oswald</u>, January 2, 1999, <gopher://freenet.akron.oh.us/h0/SIGS/JFK/FAQ/.02faq.html> (28 June 2000).

37. FTP (FILE TRANSFER PROTOCOL) SITE

Include the author's name, if available; the title; the title of the complete work, if applicable; the version and date, if known; the FTP address; and the date of access.

> 48. Sharon Michalove, "The Great Marriage Hunt: Finding a Wife in Fifteenth-Century England," September 1992, <ftp://history.cc.ukans.edu/pub/history/general/articles/michal1.art> (2 April 2000).

38. EMAIL MESSAGE

Include the author's name; the author's email address; the subject line from the posting; the date of publication; the type of communication; and the date of access.

> 49. Kyla Berry, <kberry@aasc.mo.us> "Re: Newspaper Archives," 7 May 2000, personal email (6 May 2000).

39. LISTSERV OR NEWSGROUP MESSAGE

Include the author's name; the author's email address; the subject line from the posting; the date of publication; the name of the listserv or newsgroup; and the date of access.

> 50. Claire Dehon, <dehone1@ksu.edu> "Africa Forum: Heritage and History," 30 October 1998, <http://www.h-net.msu.edu> (10 December 1999).

40. SYNCHRONOUS COMMUNICATION

Include the speaker(s), if applicable; the title and date of the event, if appropriate; the type of communication; the source; the address; and the date of communication.

```
      51. Jack Rauthier, personal communication,
The Mud Connector MUD, <mud.theinquisition.
net.5000> (3 May 2000).
```

Documentation Models for Bibliography Entries

Models for bibliography entries

Your bibliography is a list of the books, articles, and other sources you used in preparing your paper. It must include all the works you cited in your notes; it may also include other works that you consulted but did not cite. However, avoid the temptation to pad your bibliography; list only materials you did in fact use.

You should list works in your bibliography alphabetically by authors' last names. If your bibliography is long, you may wish to divide it into sections. You might, for example, create separate headings such as "Primary Sources" and "Books and Articles." If you have used manuscripts or other unpublished sources, you might list these separately as well.

Books

A typical bibliography entry for a book contains the following information:

- The author's full name, last name first, followed by a period;
- The full title of the book, underlined or italicized, followed by a period;
- The city of publication, followed by a colon;
- The name of the publisher, followed by a comma;
- The date of publication, followed by a period.

Typically, the first line of a bibliography entry is typed flush left, and subsequent lines are indented. Individual entries should be single-spaced; double-space between entries.

1. BASIC FORM FOR A BOOK

```
Mayer, Henry. All on Fire: William Lloyd Garrison
     and the Abolition of Slavery. New York: St.
     Martin's Press, 2000.
```

2. MULTIPLE WORKS BY THE SAME AUTHOR

If your bibliography includes more than one work by the same author, you should use three dashes (or three hyphens) followed by a period (---.) in place of the author's name in subsequent bibliographic entries.

```
Mayer, Henry. All on Fire: William Lloyd Garrison
     and the Abolition of Slavery. New York: St.
     Martin's Press, 2000.
```

- - -. A Son of Thunder: Patrick Henry and the
    American Republic. Charlottesville:
    University Press of Virginia, 1992.

3. TWO OR MORE AUTHORS

An entry for a book with two or more authors should begin with the name of the first author listed on the title page, last name first. The names of the other authors are given in normal order.

Bradley, James, and Ron Powers. Flags of Our
    Fathers. New York: Bantam Books, 2000.

NOTE: For books with more than three authors, you may use the first author's name followed by the Latin term "et al." ("and others") in place of the other authors' names (for example, "Doe, Jane, et al.").

4. AUTHOR'S NAME IN THE TITLE

Begin the bibliography entry with the author's name, even if it appears in the title.

Darwin, Charles. Charles Darwin's Letters: A
    Selection, 1825-1859. Edited by Frederick
    Burkhardt. Cambridge: Cambridge University
    Press, 1996.

5. ANONYMOUS WORK

If the author of a work is unknown, list the work in the bibliography by its title. If the title begins with an article (*A, An,* or *The*), alphabetize the book according to the first letter of the next word.

DK Atlas of World History. New York: Dorling
    Kindersley, 2000.

6. EDITED OR COMPILED WORK WITHOUT AN AUTHOR

List a book by the last name of the editor, translator, or compiler if no author appears on the title page (as in a collection or anthology).

Freeze, Gregory L., ed. Russia: A History. New
    York: Oxford University Press, 2000.

7. EDITED WORK WITH AN AUTHOR

For a book with an author as well as an editor, the editor's name follows the title.

```
Karsh, Efraim. Empires of the Sand: The Struggle
    for Mastery in the Middle East, 1789-1923.
    Edited by Inari Karsh. Cambridge: Harvard
    University Press, 2000.
```

8. TRANSLATED WORK

A translator's name, like an editor's, is placed after the title when an author's name is given. If a source has an editor and a translator, both should be listed.

```
Tunon, Julia. Women in Mexico: A Past Unveiled.
    Translated by Alan Hynds. Austin: University
    of Texas Press, 1999.
```

```
Vishniac, Roman. Children of a Vanished World.
    S. Mark Taper Foundation Book in Jewish
    Studies. Edited by Mara Vishniac Kohn.
    Translated by Miriam Hartman Flacks. Berke-
    ley: University of California Press, 1999.
```

9. MULTIVOLUME WORK

For a multivolume work, include the number of volumes in the bibliography entry.

```
Freedom: A Documentary History of Emancipation,
    1861-1867. 4 vols. New York: Cambridge
    University Press, 1993.
```

If you have used a single volume of a multivolume set, cite only that volume. You can do this by giving the name of the volume first:

```
The Wartime Genesis of Free Labor: The Upper
    South. Edited by Ira Berlin. Vol. 1 of
    Freedom: A Documentary History of
    Emancipation, 1861-1867. New York: Cambridge
    University Press, 1993.
```

or by giving the name of the series first:

```
Freedom: A Documentary History of Emancipation,
    1861-1867. Vol. 1, The Wartime Genesis of
    Free Labor: The Upper South. Edited by Ira
    Berlin. New York: Cambridge University
    Press, 1993.
```

If an individual volume in a multivolume work does not have its own title, specify the volume by number.

Cambridge History of American Foreign Relations.
Vol. 1. Cambridge: Cambridge University
Press, 1993.

If the volume or collection of volumes has an author, the entry should begin with the author's name (last name first), followed by a period.

10. ARTICLE IN A COLLECTION OR ANTHOLOGY

List an article in a collection or anthology by the author of the article. You may include the pages on which the article begins and ends.

Kilcup, Karen. "Nancy Ward and Early Cherokee
Women." In Native American Women's Writing,
12. Malden, Mass.: Blackwell, 2000.

11. LETTER IN A PUBLISHED COLLECTION

If you cite only one letter from a collection, you may list it as an individual letter in your bibliography.

An Expectant Mother to Eleanor Roosevelt, 2
January 1935. In America 1900-1999: Letters
of the Century. Edited by Lisa Grunwald and
Stephen J. Adler. New York: Dial Press,
1999.

However, if you cite several letters from the same collection, list only the collection.

America 1900-1999: Letters of the Century. Edited
by Lisa Grunwald and Stephen J. Adler. New
York: Dial Press, 1999.

12. EDITION OTHER THAN THE FIRST

If you are using any edition other than the first, include the edition number in your bibliography.

Chafe, William H. The Unfinished Journey: America
since World War II, 4th ed. New York: Oxford
University Press, 1999.

13. WORK IN A SERIES

A series is a set of publications on the same general subject that is supervised by an editor or group of editors. Begin the entry with the author and title of the individual work from the series. Also include the title and editor of the series.

```
Abzug, Robert H. America Views the Holocaust,
     1933-1945. Bedford Series in History and
     Culture, edited by (advisors) Natalie Zemon
     Davis and Ernest R. May. Boston: Bedford/St.
     Martin's, 1999.
```

Periodicals

A typical bibliography entry for an article in a journal includes the following information:

- The author's full name, last name first, followed by a period;
- The title of the article, in quotation marks and followed by a period;
- The name of the journal, underlined or italicized;
- The volume number, in arabic numerals;
- The date, in parentheses, followed by a colon;
- The pages on which the article begins and ends, followed by a period.

14. ARTICLE IN A JOURNAL PAGINATED BY VOLUME

Most scholarly journals are paginated consecutively throughout the volume. When citing an article from such a journal, it is not mandatory that you give the issue number.

```
Landsman, Ned C. "Nation, Migration, and the
     Province in the First British Empire:
     Scotland and the Americas, 1600-1800."
     American Historical Review 104 (1999): 463.
```

15. ARTICLE IN A JOURNAL PAGINATED BY ISSUE

If a journal paginates each issue separately, you must provide the issue number.

```
Wynn, Rhoda. "Saints and Sinners: Women and the
     Practice of Medicine throughout the Ages."
     Journal of the American Medical Association
     283, no. 5 (2000): 668.
```

NOTE: If you wish to include the month of publication, put it before the year: (March 2000). If you include the month, you do not need the issue number.

16. ARTICLE IN A POPULAR MAGAZINE

It is not necessary to give the volume number or issue number for an article in a popular magazine. If you include page numbers, they are preceded by a comma, not by a colon.

```
Elliott, Michael, and Michael Hirsh. "Learning
     the Lessons of Kosovo." Newsweek Special
     Edition, December 1999-February 2000, 22-26.
```

17. NEWSPAPER ARTICLE

If you consulted various articles from a particular newspaper, you don't have to list the articles separately in the bibliography. Instead, provide just the name of the paper and the range of dates of the issues you consulted.

```
Kansas City Star, 4 February-8 February 2000.
```

18. BOOK REVIEW

List a book review by the reviewer's last name. If the author of the review is not named, begin with the title of the review or, if the review is untitled, with the words "Review of."

```
Cooper, Ilene. Review of Nat Turner's Slave
     Rebellion in American History, by Judith
     Edwards. Booklist 96 (2000): 1093.

Review of A Middle East Mosaic: Fragments of
     Life, Letters and History, edited by Bernard
     Lewis. Publishers Weekly, 24 March 2000, 80.
```

Public documents

The same information should be provided as for notes (see pp. 76–78). In a paper on United States history, you may omit "United States" or "U.S." as the country in which a document was issued if it is clear in context.

19. PRESIDENTIAL PAPERS

Entries for these papers often begin with and are alphabetized by the president's name.

```
Eisenhower, Dwight D. Public Papers of the
     Presidents of the United States: Dwight D.
     Eisenhower, 1953. Washington, D.C.: GPO,
     1960.
```

20. EXECUTIVE DEPARTMENT DOCUMENT

Entries for these documents begin with the issuing department's name.

```
U.S. General Accounting Office. Desert Shield and
     Desert Storm Reports and Testimonies,
     1991-93. Washington, D.C.: General
     Accounting Office, 1994.
```

```
U.S. Department of State. Belarus. Background
     Notes Series, no. 10344.
```

21. TESTIMONY BEFORE A COMMITTEE

If you cite or consult a transcript of testimony before a committee, begin the entry with the name of the committee.

```
House Committee on Veterans' Affairs. Radiation
     Research in the VA Involving Human Subjects:
     Hearing before the Committee on Veterans'
     Affairs. 103d Cong., 2d sess. Washington,
     D.C.: GPO, 1994.
```

22. CONGRESSIONAL COMMITTEE PRINT

Entries for these research reports should include the print number or date.

```
U.S. Congress, Senate Committee on Foreign
     Relations. Inter-American Foundation
     Projects in Argentina and Haiti: A Staff
     Report to the Committee on Foreign
     Relations. 106th Cong., 2d sess., 2000, 110.
```

23. TREATY

Begin the entry with the name of the issuing agency.

```
U.S. Department of State. "Jay Treaty," 19
     November 1794. TIAS no. 105. United States
     Treaties and Other International Agreements,
     vol. 2.
```

(See p. 77 for information about the TIAS number.)

24. UNITED STATES CONSTITUTION

If you cite the Constitution in your paper, you do not need to include it in your bibliography.

Other sources

25. UNPUBLISHED THESIS OR DISSERTATION

List an unpublished thesis or dissertation by its author's last name.

```
Nemes, Robert James. "Between Reform and
      Revolution: Associations, Culture and
      Politics in Budapest, 1800-1849." Ph.D.
      diss., Columbia University, 1999.
```

26. ILLUSTRATION

For an illustration in a printed text, give the authors, title, city, publisher, and year.

```
Time/CBS News. People of the Century. New York:
      Simon & Schuster, 1999.
```

27. SOUND RECORDING

List a sound recording by the composer's last name or, for a collection or an anonymous work, by the title of the recording. Include the recording company and number if they are provided.

```
Holst, Gustav. The Planets. Royal Philharmonic
      Orchestra. André Previn. Telarc compact disc
      80133.
```

```
Virtuoso Recorder Music. Amsterdam Loeki Stardust
      Quartet. Decca compact disc 414 277-2.
```

28. FILM OR VIDEOCASSETTE

After the film title, include the name of the producer and director, the playing time, the production company, the date, and the medium.

```
The Civil War. Produced by Ken Burns. 11 hours.
      PBS Video, 1990. 9 videocassettes.
```

29. INTERVIEW

List an interview under the name of the person interviewed and provide the date of the interview.

```
McVeigh, Timothy. Interviewed by Ed Bradley.
      60 Minutes. Columbia Broadcasting System, 26
      March 2000.
```

30. PERSONAL COMMUNICATION

Because your reader will not have access to personal interviews you conducted or letters you received, you do not need to list these sources of information in your bibliography.

31. REFERENCE WORKS AND THE BIBLE

Well-known reference works and the Bible are usually not included in bibliographies.

32. INDIRECT SOURCE

If material you have taken from one source originally appeared in another source and you have not consulted the original yourself, your bibliography entry should begin with the original source but must include your own source for the information. The page numbers from both sources should be included.

```
Knoles, George Harmon. The Jazz Age Revisited:
     British Criticism of American Civilization
     during the 1920s, 31. Stanford: Stanford
     University Press, 1955. Quoted in C. Vann
     Woodward, The Old World's New World (Oxford:
     Oxford University Press, 1991), 46.
```

Electronic sources

33. WEB SITE

```
Martin, A. "Napoleon Bonaparte," n.d., <http://
     www.napoleon1er.com/> (22 March 2000).
```

34. GOPHER SITE

```
Stahl, P. J. "Questions Concerning Oswald's
     Personality," The Real FAQ: Questions
     Concerning Lee Harvey Oswald, 2 January
     1999, <gopher://freenet.akron.oh.us/h0/SIGS/
     JFK/FAQ/.02faq.html> (28 June 2000).
```

35. FTP (FILE TRANSFER PROTOCOL) SITE

```
Michalove, Sharon. "The Great Marriage Hunt:
     Finding a Wife in Fifteenth-Century
     England," September 1992, <ftp://
     history.cc.ukans.edu/pub/history/general/
     articles/michal1.art> (2 April 2000).
```

36. EMAIL MESSAGE

```
Berry, Kyla. <kberry@aasc.mo.us> "Re: Newspaper
     Archives," 7 May 2000. Personal email (6 May
     2000).
```

37. LISTSERV OR NEWSGROUP MESSAGE

```
Dehon, Claire. <dehone1@ksu.edu> "Africa Forum:
    Heritage and History." 30 October 1998,
    <http://www.h-net.msu.edu> (10 December
    1999).
```

38. SYNCHRONOUS COMMUNICATION

```
Rauthier, Jack. Personal communication. The Mud
    Connector MUD. <mud.theinquisition.net.5000>
    (3 May 2000).
```

5f. Sample pages from a student research paper

Most of the suggestions in this book have been directed toward a single end: the production of a carefully researched, well-organized, and clearly written paper. On the following pages, you will find the title page, opening paragraphs, notes, and bibliography for one such paper.

SAMPLE TITLE PAGE

To Try a Monarch:
The Trials and Executions of
Charles I of England and Louis XVI of France

by
Lynn Chandler

History 362
Dr. Joan Kinnaird
April 24, 2000

SAMPLE PAGE   Chandler 2

On January 30, 1649, Charles I, king of
England, was beheaded. The crowd around the
scaffold greeted the sight of the severed head of
their monarch with astonished silence. After
lying in state for several days, the body was
carried "in a Hearse covered with black Velvet,
and drawn by six Horses, with four Coaches
following it. . . ."[1] to Windsor Castle, where
Charles was buried in royal estate beside Henry
VIII and Queen Jane Seymour.[2] The scene was quite
different on January 21, 1793, when another
monarch ascended the scaffold--Louis XVI, king of
the French. In place of the silence that followed
Charles's execution, Louis's decapitation was
announced with a "flourish of trumpets," and the
executioner's cry of "Thus dies a Traitor!"[3]
Contemporaries reported that the crowd surged
forward, dipped their handkerchiefs in the king's
blood, and ran through the streets shouting
"Behold the Blood of a Tyrant!"[4] The body was
wrapped in canvas and brought in a cart to the
Tuilleries, where Louis XVI, the former king of
France, was buried like a commoner.[5] These two
events, separated by almost a century and a half,
appear at first glance to be totally isolated
from each other. A careful review of both
official documents and private accounts, however,
reveals that the chief actors in the drama
surrounding the execution of Louis XVI were not
only aware of the English precedent, but referred
to it again and again in the process of choosing
their own courses of action, arguing for the
validity of their point of view, and justifying
their actions to the world.

The first clear-cut evidence that the French
were influenced by the trial and execution of
Charles I can be found in contemporary
transcripts of the trial itself. In the debate
surrounding the decision to execute the king,
those who favored leniency often cited the
English precedent to support their position.

SAMPLE END NOTES PAGE

Notes

1. England's Black Tribunal: The Tryal of King Charles the First (printed for C. Revington, at the Bible and Crown in St. Paul's Churchyard, 1737), 55.

2. For a detailed account of the trial and execution of Charles I, see C. V. Wedgewood, A Coffin for King Charles: The Trial and Execution of Charles I (New York: Time Incorporated, 1966) and Graham Edwards, The Last Days of Charles I (Stroud, Gloucestershire: Sutton Publishing, 1999).

3. Joseph Trapp, The Trial of Louis XVI (London, 1793), 205.

4. Trapp, 206.

5. Trapp, 145. For a detailed account of the trial and execution of Louis XVI, see David P. Jordan, The King's Trial: The French Revolution vs. Louis XVI (Berkeley and Los Angeles: University of California Press, 1979).

6. Michael Walzer, Regicide and Revolution: Speeches at the Trial of Louis XVI, trans. Marian Rothstein (Cambridge: Cambridge University Press, 1974), 1-89 passim.

7. Edwards, Last Days, 56.

8. Patricia Crawford, "'Charles Stuart, That Man of Blood,'" Journal of British Studies 16, no. 2 (1977): 53.

9. Wedgewood, 89.

10. Wedgewood, 110.

11. Susan Dunn, The Deaths of Louis XVI: Regicide and the French Imagination (Princeton, N.J.: Princeton University Press, 1994), 59.

12. Jordan, 121.

13. Jordan, 122.

14. John Hardman, The French Revolution Sourcebook (London: Arnold Publishers, 1999), 178.

Bibliography

Blackwell, Freida H., and Jay Losey. "The
    Execution of Charles I: History and
    Perspectives," n.d., <http://www.baylor.edu/
    ~BIC/WCIII/Essays/charles.1.html> (23 March
    2000).

Crawford, Patricia. "'Charles Stuart, That Man of
    Blood.'" Journal of British Studies 16, no.
    2 (1977): 41-61.

Dunn, Susan. The Deaths of Louis XVI: Regicide
    and the French Political Imagination.
    Princeton, N.J.: Princeton University Press,
    1994.

Edwards, Graham. The Last Days of Charles I.
    Stroud, Gloucestershire: Sutton Publishing,
    1999.

England's Black Tribunal: The Tryal of King
    Charles the First. Printed for C. Revington,
    at the Bible and Crown in St. Paul's
    Churchyard, 1737.

Hardman, John. The French Revolution Sourcebook.
    London: Arnold Publishers, 1999.

Jordan, David P. "In Defense of the King."
    Stanford French Review 1, no. 3 (1977): 325-
    338.

---. The King's Trial: The French Revolution vs.
    Louis XVI. Berkeley and Los Angeles:
    University of California Press, 1979.

Knachel, Philip A., ed. Eikon Basilike: The
    Portraiture of His Sacred Majesty in His
    Solitudes and Sufferings. Ithaca, N.Y.:
    Cornell University Press, 1966.

Trapp, Joseph. The Trial of Louis XVI. London,
    1793.

Walzer, Michael, ed. Regicide and Revolution:
    Speeches at the Trial of Louis XVI.
    Translated by Marian Rothstein. Cambridge:
    Cambridge University Press, 1974.

Wedgewood, C.V. A Coffin for King Charles: The
    Trial and Execution of Charles I. New York:
    Time Incorporated, 1966.

Appendix A
Writing Guides of Interest to Historians

The following books offer helpful guidance on stylistic matters and other writing concerns. The guides to writing in history, in addition to offering general writing advice, discuss how historians work and cover typical assignments in history, stylistic conventions, the research process, and documentation.

GENERAL WRITING GUIDES

Hacker, Diana. *A Pocket Style Manual*. 3rd ed. Boston: Bedford/St. Martin's, 2000.

Hacker, Diana. *Rules for Writers*. 4th ed. Boston: Bedford/St. Martin's, 2000.

Strunk, William, Jr., and E. B. White. *The Elements of Style*. 4th ed. New York: Macmillan, 1999.

Turabian, Kate L., Alice Bennett, and John Grossman. *A Manual for Writers of Term Papers, Theses, and Dissertations*. 6th ed. Chicago: University of Chicago Press, 1996.

University of Chicago Press. *The Chicago Manual of Style*. 14th ed. Chicago: University of Chicago Press, 1993.

GUIDES TO WRITING IN HISTORY

Benjamin, Jules R. *A Student's Guide to History*. 8th ed. Boston: Bedford/St. Martin's, 2001.

Marius, Richard. *A Short Guide to Writing about History*. 3rd ed. New York: HarperCollins, 1999.

Scott, Gregory M., Stephen M. Garrison, and Mark Hellstern. *The History Student Writer's Manual*. Upper Saddle River, N.J.: Prentice Hall, 1998.

Stephens, Henry J., Mary Jane Dickerson, and Toby Fulwiler. *Writer's Guide: History*. The Heath Writing across the Curriculum Series, Arthur W. Biddle, General Editor. Lexington, Mass.: D. C. Heath, 1987.

Storey, William Kelleher. *Writing History: A Guide for Students*. New York: Oxford University Press, 1999.

INTERNET GUIDES FOR HISTORIANS

Harnack, Andrew, and Eugene Kleppinger. *Online! A Reference Guide to Using Internet Sources*. 2000 ed. Boston: Bedford/St. Martin's, 2000.

Stull, Andrew T. *History on the Internet 1998–1999: A Prentice Hall Guide*. Adapted for history by John Paul Rossi. New Jersey: Prentice Hall, 1999.

Trinkle, Dennis A., and Scott A. Merriman. *The History Highway 2000: A Guide to Internet Resources*. 2nd edition. Armonk, N.Y.: M. E. Sharpe, 2000.

Appendix B
Guide to Resources in History

by Susan Craig, Trinity College

While doing research in history, you will need to collect evidence and find commentary that helps you interpret it. Your library and the Internet offer many tools that can help you track down primary and secondary sources and answer questions that arise as you learn more about your topic. This appendix suggests selected indexes, references, periodicals, and sources of primary documents. It also offers a sampler of electronic sources available through the Internet. The materials listed here are not available at all libraries, but they give you an idea of the range of resources available. Remember, too, that librarians are an extremely helpful resource. They know their own collections well and can direct you to useful materials throughout your research process.

Library resources

INDEXES

America: History and Life. Santa Barbara, Calif.: ABC-CLIO, 1964–.
> Abstracts of articles on the history of the United States and Canada published throughout the world, as well as articles dealing with current U.S. culture. Includes book reviews and abstracts of dissertations. Available in CD-ROM and online formats.

Historical Abstracts. Santa Barbara, Calif.: ABC-CLIO, 1955–.
> Abstracts from world periodical literature covering world history from 1450. Scope excludes the United States and Canada. From 1971, selectively indexes book reviews, monographs, and dissertations. Available in CD-ROM and online formats.

Humanities Index. New York: H. W. Wilson, 1974–.
> An index to international magazines and journals in the field of humanities, including history. From 1907 to 1974, this index was in a combined title, *Social Sciences and Humanities Index.* Available in CD-ROM and online formats.

Readers' Guide to Periodical Literature. New York: H. W. Wilson, 1900–.

> An index to popular magazines published in the United States, beginning in 1900. An earlier index, *Poole's Index to Periodical Literature*, covers 1802–1906. Available in CD-ROM and online formats.

GUIDES AND BIBLIOGRAPHIES

American Historical Association's Guide to Historical Literature. 3rd ed. New York: Oxford University Press, 1995.

> Over 27,000 citations to worldwide historical literature, arranged in sections covering theory, international history, and regional history. An indispensable guide updated to include current trends in historical research published between 1961 and 1992.

Encyclopedia of Historians and Historical Writing. Chicago: Fitzroy Dearborn, 1999.

> A two-volume international guide to influential historians and historical debates. Includes biographies of individuals born no later than 1945, essays on nations and geographical regions, and topical essays.

The History Highway: A Guide to Internet Resources. Armonk, N.Y.: Sharpe, 1997.

> A general introduction to the skills and tools necessary to navigate the Internet. Offers detailed information about thousands of references to history Web sites.

International Medieval Bibliography. Leeds: University of Leeds, 1967–.

> Semiannual volumes cover the whole range of medieval sources, indexing periodical literature and monographs.

Sources of Information for Historical Research. New York: Neal-Schuman, 1994.

> A guide to major reference works, including online databases, to assist researchers in the retrieval of historical information.

Term Paper Resource Guide to Twentieth-Century United States History. Westport, Conn.: Greenwood Press, 1999.

> Organized by one hundred important historical events (from the Spanish-American War to the North American Free Trade Agreement), this guide provides reference, biographical, periodical, audiovisual, and Internet sources, along with suggestions for term paper topics.

United States History: A Selective Guide to Information Sources. Englewood, Colo.: Libraries Unlimited, 1994.

> Arranged topically, over 1,000 annotated entries describe reference, bibliographic, and biographical sources in U.S. history.

Voices of the Spirit: Sources for Interpreting the African-American Experience. Chicago: American Library Association, 1995.

> An annotated bibliography of classic and contemporary resources in African American history. Focuses on reference books, general history books, traveling exhibits, and videotapes.

OVERVIEWS OF TOPICS IN HISTORY

Africana: The Encyclopedia of the African and African American Experience. New York: Basic Civitas Books, 1999.

Articles on the history of each African nation and every major cultural, political, and religious movement in Africa and the New World.

The American Revolution, 1775–1783: An Encyclopedia. New York: Garland, 1993.

A two-volume set that provides over 800 comprehensive summaries of military and naval developments of the era.

Black Women in America: An Historical Encyclopedia. Brooklyn: Carlson, 1993.

Biographical and topical articles on over 800 African American women. Includes photographs, illustrations, bibliographies, and an extensive "Chronology of Black Women in the United States from 1619 to 1992."

Civilizations of the Ancient Near East. New York: Scribner, 1995.

A four-volume set that provides a survey of the culture and history of Egypt, Syro-Palestine, Mesopotamia, and Anatolia. Includes a "Timetable of Civilizations" and numerous illustrations and maps.

Dictionary of American History. Rev. ed. New York: Scribner, 1976.

An eight-volume encyclopedia of terms, places, and concepts in U.S. history. A supplement volume was published in 1996. Related titles include *Encyclopedia of the Confederacy* (1993) and *Encyclopedia of the North American Colonies* (1993).

Encyclopedia of African-American Culture and History. New York: Macmillan Library Reference, 1996.

A five-volume set with entries that cover African American people, places, events, concepts, and topics from 1619 to 1995.

Encyclopedia of American Social History. New York: Scribner, 1993.

Covers topics such as religion, race, gender, popular culture, regionalism, and everyday life from pre-Columbian to modern times.

Encyclopedia of Asian History. New York: Scribner, 1988.

Detailed articles on people, places, and events in Asian history. Covers Central Asia, South Asia, and the Far East.

Encyclopedia of Latin American History and Culture. New York: C. Scribner Sons, 1996.

Over 5,000 entries in five volumes cover Latin American history from earliest times to the present.

Encyclopedia of Russian History: From the Christianization of Kiev to the Break-up of the USSR. Santa Barbara, Calif.: ABC-CLIO, 1993.

A revised edition of *Companion to Russian History* (1983). Contains over 2,500 entries covering people, places, religious and political movements, intellectual ideas, and the arts.

Encyclopedia of the Holocaust. New York: Macmillan, 1990.

A four-volume set that documents the Jewish holocaust — its background, history, and impact. Includes illustrations, photographs, maps, and numerous cross-references.

Encyclopedia of the Renaissance. New York: Facts on File, 1987.

An alphabetical arrangement of short entries covering the cultural, historical, and individual achievements of the fifteenth and sixteenth centuries.

Encyclopedia of the United States in the Twentieth Century. New York: Scribner's, 1996.

An ambitious survey of American cultural, social, and intellectual history organized as broad articles arranged by topic.

Encyclopedia of the Vietnam War: A Political, Social, and Military History. Santa Barbara, Calif.: ABC-CLIO, 1998.

A three-volume comprehensive study of the wars in Vietnam that details Vietnamese history to the present; including French and U.S. involvement. Includes maps, illustrations, and a collection of relevant documents.

Encyclopedia of Women's History in America. New York: Facts on File, 1996.

Short topical and biographical entries of women central to the course of U.S. cultural, intellectual, and political history. Includes documents of importance to women's history.

Gale Encyclopedia of Native American Tribes. Detroit: Gale, 1998.

A four-volume set that provides essays on tribal history, religions, language, buildings, customs, and current tribal issues.

Japanese American History: An A–Z Reference from 1868 to the Present. New York: Facts on File, 1993.

A narrative historical overview, a chronology, and dictionary entries on Japanese American history.

Longman Handbook of Modern European History, 1763–1997. 3rd ed. New York: Longman, 1998.

A condensed single-volume work that collects chronological, statistical, and tabular data covering political, social, and economic history, as well as biographies of important individuals.

Macmillan Encyclopedia of World Slavery. New York: Macmillan Reference, 1998.

This two-volume set documents the institution of slavery on a global scale, from ancient times to the present day.

Medieval England: An Encyclopedia. New York: Garland, 1998.

Entries provide an introduction to the society and culture of England from the coming of the Anglo-Saxons in the fifth century to the turn of the sixteenth century.

New Cambridge Modern History. Cambridge: Cambridge University Press, 1957–79.

A multivolume work covering 1493 to 1945 in chronological and topical order, with detailed narrative surveys. A supplemental volume was published in 1990. Similar works by Cambridge University Press include those on ancient history, medieval history, and histories of regions and countries, such as the more recent *Cambridge History of Africa* (1990), and *Cambridge History of the Native American Peoples of the Americas* (1996).

Oxford Encyclopedia of the Modern Islamic World. New York: Oxford University Press, 1995.

A four-volume set offering articles on all facets of Muslim historical, social, political, and religious life from the end of the eighteenth century to the present.

Oxford Encyclopedia of the Reformation. New York: Oxford University Press, 1996.

A four-volume set that covers people, places, events, documents, and ideas relevant to the Reformation.

SPECIALIZED DICTIONARIES

ABC-CLIO Companion to Women's Progress in America. Santa Barbara, Calif.: ABC-CLIO, 1994.

An alphabetical record of the public milestones of women's history from 1619, including women whose achievements were unusual for their time, who championed women's rights, or who pioneered the way for others.

The Blackwell Companion to the Enlightenment. Oxford: Blackwell, 1995.

Concise entries on the music, art, literature, technological advances, and personalities from around the world that characterized the years 1720–1780.

Dictionary of American Biography. New York: Cambridge University Press, 1995.

A multivolume work that provides short biographical entries of significant Americans from colonial times through the late twentieth century.

Dictionary of Ancient History. Oxford: Blackwell, 1994.

Concise entries on the personalities, events, literature, philosophy, art, religions, and sciences in the Greco-Roman world, from 776 B.C. to A.D. 476.

Dictionary of Concepts in History. New York: Greenwood, 1996.

Essays that define historiographic concepts and describe how the concepts were formed. Contains excellent bibliographies.

Dictionary of National Biography. New York: Macmillan, 1908–09. Supplements: 1912–81.

The original twenty-two-volume set provides biographies of notable inhabitants of the British Isles and the colonies, as well as notable Americans of the colonial period. Supplements bring the records forward to 1970. Includes a cumulative index covering all entries from 1901.

Dictionary of Scandinavian History. New York: Greenwood, 1986.

Entries deal with the histories of Denmark, Finland, Iceland, Norway, and Sweden since A.D. 1000.

Dictionary of Scientific Biography. New York: Scribner, 1970–80. *Supplement II.* New York: Scribner, 1990.

Signed biographical essays on international scientists from all periods of history, covering the subject's accomplishments and place in the development of science.

Dictionary of the Middle Ages. New York: Scribner, 1982–89.

> The single most complete source covering people, events, ideas, movements, texts, and cultural features of the medieval world. This thirteen-volume set covers A.D. 500 to A.D. 1500.

Dictionary of the Russian Revolution. New York: Greenwood, 1989.

> A guide to the major institutions, people, and movements associated with the Russian Revolutions of 1917 to 1921.

Dictionary of Twentieth-Century World History. New York: Oxford University Press, 1997.

> Concise, comprehensive topical and biographical entries on all sovereign countries, historical regions, world and military leaders, movements, and treaties.

Historical Dictionary of Germany. Metuchen, N.J.: Scarecrow Press, 1994.

> Concise entries introduce significant persons, places, events, and cultural developments. Includes a detailed chronology from A.D. 9 to 1993 and an extensive bibliography.

Historical Dictionary of the American Revolution. Lanham, Md.: Scarecrow Press, 1999.

> Concise topical entries, an extensive bibliography, and a collection of important military and political documents associated with the war.

Historical Dictionary of the Elizabethan World: Britain, Ireland, Europe, and America. Phoenix: Oryx Press, 1999.

> Concise entries on the people, events, ideas, and terms relating to the Elizabethan period of British history. Contains genealogical charts; lists of archbishops, monarchs, and popes; historical literature, motion pictures, and sound recordings; Web sites; and a bibliography.

Historical Dictionary of the Progressive Era, 1890–1920. New York: Greenwood, 1988.

> Covers the people, events, organizations, legislation, and concepts in the United States between 1890 and 1920. Other titles in this series include the *Historical Dictionary of the 1920's, from World War I to the New Deal, 1919–1933* (1988) and the *Historical Dictionary of the New Deal* (1985).

ATLASES, CHRONOLOGIES, AND TIMETABLES

Atlas of Classical History. New York: Oxford University Press, 1994.

> Provides maps covering the Near East, ancient Egypt, Greece, and Rome from 1700 B.C. to A.D. 565.

Black Saga: The African-American Experience — a Chronology. Washington, D.C.: Civitas/Counterpoint, 1999.

> A chronological documentary of the African American experience from 1492 to 1994.

Chronology of European History, 15,000 B.C. to 1997. Pasadena: Salem Press, 1997.

> Chronological entries on the social, political, economic, and intellectual history of Europe.

Chronology of Hispanic-American History. New York: Gale, 1995.

Lists historical and cultural highlights of people whose origin is Mexico, Puerto Rico, Cuba, Spain, and the Spanish-speaking countries of Central and South America, beginning with pre-Columbian time (50,000 B.C.) to 1995. Includes regional histories and significant documents.

Chronology of Native American History from Pre-Columbian Times to the Present. Detroit: Gale, 1994.

A comprehensive listing of historical and cultural events involving the native peoples of North America and Canada. Includes numerous illustrations, a list of American Indian orators, historical documents, and excerpts from significant legal cases.

Chronology of the Modern World, 1763–1992. New York: Simon & Schuster, 1994.

A guide to world events and achievements highlighting such topics as political and international events, science, scholarship, religion, fine arts, and sports.

Chronology of Twentieth-Century Eastern Europe History. Detroit: Gale, 1994.

A concise look at Eastern Europe's major political, economic, and cultural events, arranged by countries.

Chronology of Twentieth-Century History: Ecology and the Environment. Chicago: Fitzroy Dearborn, 1997.

A two-volume chronological arrangement of key events that have shaped the environment throughout the world, from the Reclamation Act (1902) to the Environmental Protection Administration's Air Pollution Regulations (1996).

Chronology of Women's History. Westport, Conn.: Greenwood, 1994.

Chronological entries from 20,000 B.C. to A.D. 1994 highlight some of the landmarks in women's history in categories such as daily life, education, literature, science, and religion.

Chronology of World History. Santa Barbara, Calif.: ABC-CLIO, 1999.

This four-volume set covers the ancient and medieval world (3000 B.C.) to the modern world (A.D. 1998). Entries are arranged chronologically and grouped into topical categories.

Chronology of World Slavery. Santa Barbara, Calif.: ABC-CLIO, 1999.

Examines the institution of slavery throughout history and across cultures with topical articles and a collection of primary documents.

Historical Atlas of Britain. Dover, N.H.: A. Sutton in association with the National Trust, 1994.

Presents a comprehensive view of British history. Includes topical essays, maps, and pictures.

Historical Atlas of Political Parties in the United States Congress, 1789–1989. New York: Macmillan, 1989.

Maps the geographic patterns of political parties for each Congress through the 100th Congress (1989), showing political affiliation for each district, Senator, and Representative.

Key Facts in Soviet History. Vol. 1, *1917 to 22 June 1941* (sometimes known as *Chronology of Soviet History*). Boston: Hall, 1990.

A chronology of people, events, speeches, resolutions, and treaties.

Rand McNally Atlas of World History. Chicago: Rand McNally, 1995.

Shows the development of human society in its physical setting through maps and text.

Smithsonian Timelines of the Ancient World. New York: Dorling Kindersley, 1993.

Starting with the origins of life and ending at A.D. 1500, this colorful volume provides geographical charts, introductory historical text, and topical articles.

The Times Atlas of World History. 4th ed. Maplewood, N.J.: Hammond, 1994.

Covers the world's past geographically.

Timetable of African American History: Five Hundred Years of Black Achievement. New York: Roundtable Press, 1994.

Makes available in chronological sequence the dates of major events in African American history from the fifteenth century to 1994.

The Timetables of History. 3rd ed. New York: Simon & Schuster, 1991.

Covers the arts, politics, religion, science and technology, and daily life year by year, from ancient times to the present. Other works in this series include *Timetables of Science* (1988) and *Timetables of Women's History* (1994).

World in Turmoil: An Integrated Chronology of the Holocaust and World War II. New York: Greenwood, 1991.

A day-by-day chronology, from 1933 to 1948, covering the most important political and diplomatic events affecting world and Jewish history.

Where to find primary sources

There are many ways to find primary sources for historical research. You can search your library catalog using the names of historical figures as authors, conduct an online search, or consult anthologies of documents covering particular themes or periods in history. The following special materials can help you find useful primary sources.

THE PRESS

African American History in the Press, 1851–1899. Detroit: Gale, 1996.

Chronologically arranged articles, editorials, and cartoons from major newspapers of the nineteenth century provide a look at positive and negative portrayals of African Americans.

American Periodicals Series, 1741–1900. Ann Arbor: University Microfilms International, 1979.

Microfilm collection covering periodicals from the colonial period to the turn of the twentieth century.

Herstory. Berkeley, CA: Women's History Research Center.

> Microfilm collection covering alternative feminist periodicals published between 1960 and 1980. Offers an interesting documentary history of the women's movement.

The New York Times. New York: H. J. Raymond & Co. 1851–.

> The *Times* has been called "the newspaper of record" for its coverage of key events. Many libraries have it on microfilm going back to the first issue in 1851. An index to the *Times* itself constitutes a detailed chronology of events. Available online at <http://www.nytimes.com>.

Times. London, England: Times Newspapers Ltd., 1788–.

> This newspaper is available in microfilm at some libraries. An index covers the *Times* and its predecessor, the *Daily Universal Register* (1785–1787), from 1785 to the present. Available online at <www.the-times.co.uk>.

DIARIES, PAMPHLETS, AND BOOKS

Afro-American Pamphlets. Pts. 1–3, 1827–1948.

> A set of 149 pamphlets by influential African Americans of educational, political, and social significance.

American Culture Series.

> A microfilm set, including a subject index, featuring books and pamphlets published between 1493 and 1875.

American Diaries: An Annotated Bibliography of Published American Diaries and Journals. Detroit: Gale, 1983–87. Vol. 1, *Diaries Written from 1492–1864* (1983). Vol. 2, *Diaries Written from 1865–1980* (1987).

> A major source for determining the existence of published diaries and journals. Over 6,000 entries from all fifty states and Spanish American sites arranged chronologically and then alphabetically by author.

American Women's Diaries from the Collection of the American Antiquarian Society. New Canaan, Conn.: Readex Corp., 1984–.

> A set of microfilmed diaries kept by women from New England and the southern and western United States.

Check List of American Revolutionary War Pamphlets in the Newberry Library. Chicago: Newberry Library, 1922.

> Early editions and contemporary reprints of American and English political and military pamphlets from 1750 to 1786.

Early English Books, 1475–1640. Early English Books, 1641–1700. Ann Arbor: UMI Press.

> A vast collection of early books on microfilm, with indexes.

Latin American Pamphlets from the Yale University Library. New York: Clearwater, 1985.

> A microfiche set of selected documents from Mexico and Peru from 1600 to 1900.

PUBLIC DOCUMENTS

Many libraries house collections of state, federal, and United Nations documents. These papers — which include committee reports, agency records, and transcripts of hearings and speeches — provide a particularly detailed record of public life. If your library does not have a documents collection, you might be able to borrow documents from a regional government documents depository. The following are some useful series.

CIS U.S. Serial Set, 1789–1969. Washington, D.C.: Congressional Information Service, 1975–79.

> A vast compilation of a multitude of congressional documents, beginning with the first session of Congress in 1789. Some libraries have this set in microfiche.

Congressional Record. Washington, D.C.: GPO, 1874–.

> Covers debates and proceedings of Congress. Earlier series were called *Debates and Proceedings* (generally known as *Annals of Congress* (1789–1824), *Register of Debates* (1824–1837), and *Congressional Globe* (1833–1873)). Similar records exist for other countries; for example, proceedings of the English Parliament can be found in *Hansard's Parliamentary Debates*.

Foreign Relations of the United States. Diplomatic Papers. Washington, D.C.: GPO, 1861–.

> A collection of documents, including diplomatic papers, correspondence, and memoranda, that provides a detailed record of U.S. foreign policy.

Public Papers of the Presidents of the United States. Washington, D.C.: GPO, 1909–.

> Includes major documents issued by the executive branch from Hoover's administration to the present. Many sets of papers from earlier presidencies have been published as well.

LOCAL HISTORY COLLECTIONS

State and county historical societies often house a wealth of historical documents. Consider using their resources; you may find that you are the first to work with their materials.

Internet resources

The Internet is a medium of increasing importance for research. Internet discussion lists give historians a means of engaging in wide-ranging email conversations about such focused topics as women's history, ethnic history, and African history. You can post questions, raise issues, or simply eavesdrop as historians communicate informally.

The Internet is also an increasingly useful place to find primary sources. You can view photographs and drawings, play audio recordings of speeches or U.S. Supreme Court arguments, or find historical documents that you can print or save to your own computer.

As you use the Internet for research, be sure to assess the value of the material you find (see p. 19) and to document where you found it (see p. 57).

The Web sites listed below are current as of May 2000 and represent a sampling of the history sources available.

Internet search tools

SEARCH ENGINES

Search engines are programs that locate Internet sources containing the search terms that you provide. Because they seek matches based exclusively on the words you enter and don't screen for quality, they often produce vast numbers of irrelevant or useless results. They work best when you have a fairly specific topic.

AltaVista. <http://www.altavista.com>
> Allows simple and advanced searching and searching for images, audio, and video media.

FAST Search. <http://www.ussc.alltheweb.com>
> Allows simple and advanced searching, easy phrase searching, as well as language and domain filters.

Google. <http://www.google.com>
> Produces relevant results that match all of your search terms. Includes limited search directory features and indexes history under "Society & Culture."

HotBot. <http://www.hotbot.lycos.com>
> Allows simple and detailed advanced searching, easy phrase searching, domain and language filters, and searching for images, audio, and visual media. Includes limited search directory features and indexes history under "Society."

METASEARCH ENGINES

Metasearch engines run search terms through several search engines at once.

InferenceFind. <http://www.infind.com>
> InferenceFind sends your search to fifty-one search engines and returns the results in organized topical clusters.

MetaCrawler. <http://www.metacrawler.com>
> Sends your search to a number of different search engines at once. Describe your topic with a few words or a phrase, and select an option to search for all the words in any order or to search for a phrase for best results.

DIRECTORIES

Search directories list Internet sites organized in some fashion, usually by subject. Sometimes a good directory will lead you to information more quickly than a search engine, especially if your topic is fairly broad. History subjects are not consistently indexed. They can be listed under such headings as "Humanities," "Social Science," "Regional," and "Cultural."

About. <http://www.about.com>
  Indexes history under "Education."

Lycos. <http://www.lycos.com>
  Indexes history under "Society & Culture."

Yahoo! <http://www.yahoo.com>
  Indexes history under "Social Science."

INTERNET SITES FOR GENERAL RESEARCH PURPOSES

American Memory: Historical Collections for the National Digital Library. <http://memory.loc.gov/ammem/amhome.html>
  Over sixty multimedia collections of digitized documents, photographs, recorded sound, moving pictures, and text highlighting important American historical events.

Ancient Egypt. <http://www.memst.edu/egypt/main.html>
  The University of Memphis Institute of Egyptian Art and Archaeology Web site that includes a color tour of a dozen ancient Egyptian sites and links to other Egyptian sites.

Eighteenth-Century Resources. <http://andromeda.rutgers.edu/~jlynch/18th/history.html>
  Covers Internet resources on all aspects of eighteenth-century life, including history, arts, politics, and religion. Includes links to full-text electronic texts.

Encyclopaedia Britannica. < www.britannica.com>
  The classic encyclopedia with links to useful Web sites, journal articles, and books.

EuroDocs: Primary Historical Documents from Western Europe. < http://library.byu.edu/~rdh/eurodocs>
  Provides links to Western European (mainly primary) historical documents, organized by country and period.

Historical Text Archives. <http://www.geocities.com/Athens/Forum/9061/index.html>
  An extensive collection of historical documents in electronic format from several countries, including the United States, and several topical areas.

The History Net: Where History Lives on the Web <http://www.thehistorynet.com>
  Links to numerous sites on all aspects of history, including links to selected electronic journals, such as *British Heritage*, *Military History Quarterly*, *Women's History*, and *World War II*. Can be searched by publication title and by topical areas.

History/Social Studies for K–12 Teachers. <http://www.execpc.com/~dboals/boals.html>
  Encourages the use of the Web as a teaching and learning tool. Includes links to general, non-Western, European, and American history sources and dozens more.

Horus' Web Links to History Resources. <http://www.ucr.edu/h-gig>
  Introduces a diversity of educational and research resources

that are available on the Web but are not ordinarily consulted by historians to supplement disciplinary historical research.

Internet History Sourcebooks Project. <http://www.fordham.edu/halsall>

Collections of public-domain and copy-permitted historical texts presented for educational use. Includes separate "Internet Sourcebooks" on ancient, medieval, and modern history and "Subsidiary Sourcebooks" on African, East Asian, Indian, Islamic, Jewish, women's, global, and gay and lesbian history, history of science, and many more links.

Keeping America Informed. United States Government Printing Office. <http://www.access.gpo.gov>

GPO Access provides links to federal government information from the legislative, executive, and judicial branches and regulatory agencies, as well as links to such publications as the *Code of Federal Regulations* and *Congressional Record.*

NetSERF: The Internet Connection to Medieval Resources. < http://netserf.cua.edu/default.cfm>

Links to numerous sites on various aspects of medieval life, including history, arts, culture, literature, music, religion, and women. Includes a "Research Center" with information on associations, conferences, journals, and teaching materials. This site is under redesign, and its Web address may change.

Presidential Libraries. <http://www.nara.gov/nara/president/address.html>

Provides links to all ten of the presidential libraries of the National Archives and Records Administration.

Rulers. <http://www.geocities.com/Athens/1058/rulers.html>

Contains lists of heads of state and government of all countries and territories, usually going back to at least 1800.

WWW Virtual Library's History Central Catalogues. <http://www.ukans.edu/history/VL>

A vast list of links to sites of interest to historians, arranged alphabetically by general topic, including general research methods and materials, eras and epochs, historical topics, and geographical regions.

INTERNET SITES OF SPECIAL INTEREST

Some Web sites are designed to help you discover and use different kinds of Internet resources. The following sites can put you in touch with electronic discussion groups and with electronic library catalogs.

Directory of Scholarly and Professional E-Conferences. <http://www.n2h2.com/KOVACS>

This site lists and describes discussion groups of various types, including email discussion groups, newsgroups, and inter-active MOOs (multiuser domains, object-oriented) and MUDs (multiuser domains; programs that create spaces on the network in which participants can simultaneously move around and manipulate objects). Emphasis is on discussion groups that are academic or professional. Includes instructions on how to access these e-conferences.

Library of Congress. <http://lcweb.loc.gov>

    Allows searching the catalogs and collections of the Library of Congress. Includes the American Memory Project, an Online Gallery of Exhibitions (with text and illustrations), and a legislative information search directory (THOMAS).

Library Web-Based OPACs. <http://www.lights.com/webcats/>

    An international directory of online library catalogs available through the Web. Indexes by geography and library-type make it easy to find a library of interest.

ELECTRONIC JOURNALS AND MAGAZINES

An increasing number of periodicals are available in electronic format on the Internet. Some contain an entire issue, others provide access to selective articles, and others just list citations to the print version. Your library may subscribe to electronic versions of print journals, making them available from any computer connected to the Internet.

Here is a good place to locate electronic periodicals by title and by disciplinary area:

Internet Public Library: Online Serials. <http://www.ipl.org/reading/serials>

    This collection contains over 2,300 electronic titles that can be searched or browsed by subject or by title. Newspapers can be found separately in the "Newspapers" section.

The following titles are some of those that are available in electronic format:

American History at *TheHistoryNet.* <http:www.thehistorynet. com/AmericanHistory>

American Quarterly. <http://muse.jhu.edu/press/journals/aq/aq.html>

Canadian Journal of History. <http://www.usask.ca/history/cjh>

History Today. < http://www.historytoday.com/index.cfm>

Journal of African History. <http://www.journals.cup.org/owa_dba/owa/issues_in_journal?jid=AFH>

The Medieval Review (formerly *Bryn Mawr Medieval Review*). <http://www.hti.umich.edu/b/bmr/tmr.html>

World War II. <http://www.thehistorynet.com/WorldWarII>